THE BLACK JEWS OF HARLEM

Sourcebooks in Negro History

HOWARD BROTZ

The Black Jews

of Harlem

NEGRO NATIONALISM AND THE
DILEMMAS OF NEGRO LEADERSHIP

SCHOCKEN BOOKS · NEW YORK

For my mother

and

to the memory of my father

PREFACE TO THE 1970 EDITION

THIS BOOK deals with what a number of critics have pointed out are two virtually separate themes. But given the nature of the subject, a unity could not be forced or imposed upon it without doing an injustice to its concreteness and fullness. The book is about a religious group whose members claim to be Jews but who, at the same time, do not deny an ethnic or racial affiliation to another group whom they regard as so-called Negroes. As such their experience is bound to have implications both for the Jewish world and for the black, Negro, or so-called Negro world which are different and unrelated to each other.

As for the first there is almost nothing I can add to the details described within, for while I visit the group from time to time, distance has made impossible any kind of sustained contact. One development, which I had been expecting to happen for some time, has finally taken place. A similar group of people, originating in Chicago and numbering no more than forty, arrived at the Tel Aviv airport requesting admission as immigrant Jews. They came from Liberia, where they had lived for a while but where they had not been happy. As one of the men stated in a television interview in Tel Aviv, "It is difficult to be Jewish in Liberia." The Israeli authorities, after a certain amount of deliberation about the exact nature of their status, sent them to a kibbutz; and one will be interested to learn how they fare.

As to implications for the black world, which perhaps constitute the fundamental thrust of this study, one can hardly fail to be struck by the fact that what was years ago an exotic theme at the margin of Negro society has become vocal opinion in the recent past. A whole generation of students now rejects the identification "Negro," insisting upon the term "black." But this was all thought out forty years ago by the Black Jews, and kindred groups, who asserted that the term "Negro" is a badge of slavery. The emphasis upon communal power, furthermore, in the sense of communal achievements and solidarity, which is also a vocal theme today, was a persistent standpoint of these sects from the beginning. This is in no way to impute a direct causal connection between the revaluations of the sects and the later popularizations. It makes more sense to look at the sects as having articulated a response to a situation that under the pressure of latent events became more widely seen and felt. Essentially, this is the perception of the inadequacy or partial validity of "integrationism" as a doctrinaire dogma.

This much would seem to place the Black Jews squarely in the camp of what is called black nationalism. Yet a doctrinaire separatism, so commonly regarded as intrinsic to this nationalism is not a feature of this group. They have a communal life centered around their distinctive religious worship. But their "separatism" does not go beyond this, which is the normal attribute of any self-sustaining group. They have numerous white visitors and friends. In fact, one may see in all this an inwardly oriented nationalism pointing to the eternal significance of two principles that produce dignity and contentment. The first is the refusal to run away from oneself, which is implied in raising the question of who we are rather than in the answers to it. The second is self-help, directed toward a decent life, as the most solid basis of independence.

Now black or Negro opinion in the United States is in something of a crisis because, among other reasons, it has gone as far as it can on the old premises which it adapted and shaped in the struggle for civil rights. Where it is going from now on is thus of the keenest interest. It is unlikely that conversion to Judaism or Islam will be an option pursued by many people. If this is the way the sects have normalized their blackness to themselves, it must remain their private and sectarian concern. What is true of this is also true of the attempt to project a black culture as contrasted with reflection about black experience, which is in some respects different from and in other respects exactly like that of other peoples and groups. What is, however, not at all sectarian is the degree to which these sects have perceived the general foundations of self-respect underlying any people. It is in this light that they become a suggestion for the future, which is closer to the present than it was a half-dozen years ago.

HOWARD BROTZ

Hamilton, Ontario
January 1970

ACKNOWLEDGMENTS

MY INTEREST in the Black Jews began with a study of this group which I made when I was a graduate student at the University of Chicago. I should like to acknowledge the generous help given to me at that time by Professors Herbert Blumer, Everett Hughes, Edward Shils, and the late Professors E. Franklin Frazier and Louis Wirth. In the preparation of the present manuscript I have benefited much from conversations with my colleagues at Smith College, particularly Professors Stanley Elkins, Margaret Shook and Richard Slobodin. Professors Joan Bramwell, Donald Sheehan, and Leo Weinstein read the manuscript and made many suggestions from which I profited. They are, of course, in no way responsible for any errors this work might contain or the point of view it puts forth. Finally, it is with much pleasure that I make the long overdue acknowledgment of the very great debt I owe Rabbi Wentworth A. Matthew, the leader of the Commandment Keepers Congregation, who gave most generously of his time, his hospitality, and who became a good friend. Without his many kindnesses this study could never have been made. Although it is always perplexing to be held up to a sociological magnifying glass, where everything that one does and says is being observed, I should like to take this occasion to clear up the one real misunderstanding that may arise. This is that it has been impossible for me to follow Rabbi Matthew's usage regarding the word Negro. To this, however, I would say to him that whenever I use the term Negro, it means almost, if not quite, what he means by Ethiopian Hebrew.

H. B.

Northampton, Massachusetts
June 1963

CONTENTS

ix

LIST OF ILLUSTRATIONS

Between pages 72 and 73

1. The ordination of Rabbi James William by Rabbi Wentworth Matthew.

2. Rabbi William being given his priestly charge by Rabbi Matthew.

3. Elder Harold Grey from Youngstown, Ohio, delivering a lecture.

4. Rabbi Small (*far left*) with the elders of the Congregation.

5. Rabbi Matthew praying over his wife.

6. (*Left to right*) Rabbis Matthew, Small, and William coming from the Harlem River after *tashlikh* ceremony on Rosh ha-Shanah.

7. Rabbi Matthew with graduates of the Hebrew school and elders (*in white*).

8. Rabbi Matthew addresses the graduates.

9. Rabbi McKethen, a representative of the Brooklyn group.

10. The Congregation attending Hebrew school graduation.

11. Rabbis Small and Matthew pose with cake commemorating Matthew's 74th birthday and the 50th anniversary of the Commandment Keepers.

12. (*Left to right*) A Commandment Keeper from Jamaica, Rabbi Small, Mrs. Matthew, Rabbi Matthew, all attending the 50th anniversary celebration.

Permission to reproduce the photographs listed above is gratefully acknowledged to Rabbi Wentworth A. Matthew.

BEGINNINGS

AS EARLY AS 1900, Negro preachers were traveling through the Carolinas preaching the doctrine that the so-called Negroes were really the lost sheep of the House of Israel. There is no reason to think, however, that such reflections did not begin much earlier, in fact during slavery itself, when the more imaginative and more daring of the slaves began to wonder about the very human question of who they really were and where they really came from. In 1800, a well-planned insurrection of slaves, under the leadership of a slave named Gabriel, was discovered near Richmond, Virginia. Franklin Frazier's account of this event notes that Gabriel not only must have been an exceptional person as indicated by the thoroughness of his planning, but in addition made use of the Bible to impress upon the Negroes that they as the Israelites could throw off the yoke of slavery and that God would come to their aid.[1]

This points to a fact of central significance for this study: that the type of radical Protestantism which became the religious tradition of the slaves, and which in

its essence conceived of itself as a return to the literal
word of God, revealed in both Testaments and accessible
in the vernacular to all who could read, elicited on its
fringes an eccentric tradition in which the Old Testament
not only became held in honor equal to that of the New
but in fact became more venerated and even opposed to
the New Testament where they came in conflict. This was
not, to be sure, a tradition in the literal sense with the
continuity of an established orthodoxy. It is rather to be
understood as a series of attempts, beginning in the
seventeenth century, to think through and act upon con-
clusions drawn from reflection on the Bible which the
freedom of this tradition permitted and stimulated and
which kept recurring so long as the Biblical cosmogony
enjoyed an undisputed status in popular opinion.

In this tradition one may distinguish two foci that
correspond to the two subject matters of the Bible itself;
namely, law and narrative. The first comprehended what
the Bishop of Exeter in 1600 complained of in his diocese
as "Jewism." Extreme Puritans who contended that the
"old dispensation" was binding had reverted to such practices as circumcision and the seventh-day Sabbath. In
1635, Mary Chester was prosecuted for "teaching the distinction of meats." Some of the followers of the Puritan
John Traske, to avoid persecution, settled in Amsterdam
where they joined the synagogue. Akin to this was a proposal to conduct the government by a council of seventy
members in imitation of the ancient Sanhedrin.[2]

The other focus, arising out of a fascination with the
narrative of the Bible, comprehended a vast and mis-
cellaneous array of speculations about history in which

the text of the Bible was invoked in the most curious ways. In these speculations we see the first intellectual, in contrast with moral or political, impact of the enlightenment or the "publication" of science upon the popular mind and the problem in it which still plagues us today. This is the transformation of science or philosophy into popularized pseudo science by half-educated people— which not merely degrades science but, in the extreme, can even threaten to supplant it. Indeed, the use of the Bible to prove crackpot historical theories that were "projected" in the atmosphere surrounding the establishment of the Royal Society might be called the popular social science or natural history of the seventeenth century. One line of thought was concerned with origins and with the fate of the ten lost tribes of Israel. In 1650 there appeared a book by Thomas Thorowgood called *Jewes in America, or, Probabilities that the Americans are of that Race*. This was followed two years later by a book of Hamon L'Estrange the elder called *Americans No Jewes, or Improbabilities that the Americans Are of That Race;* this proposition was still being written about at least as late as 1836.[3]

Another line of thought was oriented toward the future in predictions about the restoration of the Jews. In 1650, for example, Thomas Tany, a London silversmith, discovered that he was a Jew of the tribe of Reuben and announced the imminent rebuilding of the Temple at Jerusalem with himself as High Priest.[4] In the next century this theme acquired a new lease of life in the career of Richard Brothers (1757–1824).[5] Brothers, a former naval lieutenant, contended that he was a descendant of

David and the nephew of God and announced on May 12, 1792, that the time was come for the fulfillment of the prophecies of the seventh chapter of Daniel. In the year 1798 the complete restoration of the Jews was to take place, Jerusalem was then to become the capital of the world, and Brothers was to be revealed as the prince and ruler of the Jews and the governor of all nations. Although Brothers, it is true, was placed for a time in a lunatic asylum, he did have a number of respectable supporters—including one member of Parliament—and many people sold their goods preparing to accompany him to his New Jerusalem which was to be built on both sides of the River Jordan. Brothers is also of interest as the principal founder of the theory of Anglo-Israelism (which did have seventeenth-century anticipations). In 1822 he published his *Correct Account of the Invasion of England by the Saxons,* proving that the English were the descendants of the lost ten tribes of Israel.[6] This theme, which is still alive in England and even in America, had a considerable development in the nineteenth century. As Joseph Jacobs has shown, this theory rests upon an extremely literal interpretation of the Old Testament prophecies which are seen as fulfilled in the facts of English history. For example, it is pointed out among other things that in the prophecies Israel will change his name (Hos. 1:9), be numberless (Hos. 1:10), dwell in islands (Isa. 24:15) to the north (Jer. 3:12) and west (Isa. 24:15) with colonies and be the chief of the nations. It was further prophesied that the isles (the term for which in the Hebrew original means "coasts" or "distant lands") would become too small for Israel (Isa. 49:19) and that Israel should be a nation and a company of nations (Gen. 35:11). As Jacob states it, the Anglo-Israelites at the turn of the century triumphantly asked, "What nation save England corresponds to all these prophetic signs?" [7]

This much may suffice to show the prototypes of the "Judaistic" impulses which were to recur and be transformed into a new pattern among Negroes. But one other point remains to be discussed. On the whole, these seventeenth- and eighteenth-century developments look at first sight very much like the doings of fanatics, mystics, and cranks, who were concerned merely with things which, in the words of Locke, "were in their own nature indifferent." That is to say, their use of the Bible did not seem to be connected with any explicit social or political question. But alienation from the established conventions and opinions of society—no matter how indifferent these established opinions may seem from an impartial standpoint—can never be wholly politically neutral; this of course is all the more so when they are regarded as the foundation of a social order. One is immediately reminded of the invocation of the Bible in the Army Debates of 1647 to justify a redistribution of property and a natural right to political equality as well as of the religious passion of the Independents in the Parliamentary Army who looked with admiration on the fact that Samuel had hewed Agag to pieces.[8]

All this is very much intertwined with what was discussed above as the "eccentric tradition" in radical Protestantism. And future research might show that even among the speculative eccentrics mentioned, there was a much greater degree of alienation from the political institutions of the society than might seem at first sight to be the case. Certainly if one looks at the writings of the one man in this tradition who appears to have been a genuine lunatic, namely, Richard Brothers, one sees that mixed in with his prophecies about the millennium is a praise of the French Revolution as a judgment of God. The second book of his, *A Revealed Knowledge of the Prophecies and Times*, is subtitled "Containing, with other great and remarkable things, the sudden and perpetual fall of the Turkish, German, and Russian Empires." In this work, published in 1797, he asserted that the death of Louis XVI as well as the perpetual abolition of the French monarchy was prophesied in the seventh chapter of Daniel; and at a time when England was at war with republican France, he writes in an open letter to the Prime Minister, "Will England continue this war any longer against a people that has the judgment of God in their favor?" These examples suggest that a rejection of the established political order may be as essential an element in the prototypical forms of what re-emerged among Negroes as is the free use of the Bible itself.

We see then that in the world centered upon a veneration for the Bible as the literal word of God lay both the contents of and the freedom for the kind of innovation by Negroes in America which is the subject of this book—specifically the freedom to move from an admiration of the Old Testament patriarchs to the view that they were one's very own ancestors. The slaves, of course, did not have the external freedom to travel or openly to propagate a doctrine which, as we shall see, had acute antislavery

implications. But they did have what Frazier aptly called
the "invisible institution" of the Negro church, that religious life that the slaves managed to create which they
did not share with their masters.[9] Even if the radical in-
novations with which we are familiar today and which
might have come out of this unsuperintended world
merely flickered and died without any evidence of social
effects, one is nonetheless bound to give due respect to
the impress that the Old Testament had upon the folk
culture of the Negro. The parallelism that he was able to
draw between his own bondage and that of the ancient
Hebrews who had once before been rescued from bondage has had, as is readily familiar, a powerful part in the
content of his song. As we shall see, the inward dignity
that he was able to acquire by conceiving of himself as
a descendant of the patriarchs is a central theme of the
Black Jews.

If, then, the primary vehicle of the view that the
Negroes are really the Hebrews of the Bible lay in their
own Protestant religious tradition, there were two stimuli
precipitating this view present among Negro preachers
around the turn of the century. The first was the re-
crudescence of popularized racism among Southern ex-
tremists in novels, plays, tracts, and speechmaking. The
decade 1900-1910 witnessed the publication of such books
as *The Negro a Beast: or, In the Image of God* (1900)
and *The Negro, a Menace to Civilization* (1907). Between
1901 and 1909, Ben Tillman made countless speeches to
Chautauqua audiences in all parts of the country, ex-
pounding the view that the Negroes were "akin to the
monkey" and "an ignorant and debased and debauched

race." [10] In Woodward's judgment this upsurge of outspoken racism probably reached a wider audience during these ten years than ever before, not merely in the South but in the nation as a whole.[11] As will be apparent from Chapter II, this racism supplied the grounds, in fact the very terms, of the counterracism at work, expressed in the view that the so-called Negroes are not a race but the chosen people, as well as of a number of variant counterracist themes which emerged in Negro opinion during this period.[12]

The second such stimulus was provided by Booker T. Washington's opinions, current around the turn of the century, that Negroes would be well advised to model themselves upon Jews in a number of respects but particularly with regard to the inward pride possessed by the Jewish people throughout history. This may be more important than it seems in view of the tremendous impress, as we shall point out, that Washington's entire point of view about the Negro's need for self-perfection made upon most of these sect leaders. In one of his published statements about Jews, he says:

We have a very bright and striking example in the history of the Jews in this and other countries. There is, perhaps, no race that has suffered so much, not so much in America as in some of the countries in Europe. But these people have clung together. They have had a certain amount of unity, pride, and love of race; and, as the years go on, they will be more and more influential in this country—a country where they were once despised, and looked upon with scorn and derision. It is largely because the Jewish race has had faith in itself. Unless the Negro learns more and more to imitate the Jew in these matters, to have faith in himself, he cannot expect to have any high degree of success.[13]

In more popularized forms this quickly degenerated into
a simple admiration of the Jews for being able to make
money:

Do you know the reason why a Jew moves into a colored
neighborhood? It's because he knows that colored folks don't
use their brains. Only a small minority of us use our minds.
And if you don't stop and use your own brain and think for
yourself, somebody else will use it for you and take advantage
of you.[14]

But to put aside any further discussion of these ultimate roots and influences, organized congregations styling
themselves "Black Jews" do not appear until about 1915,
in Washington, Philadelphia, New York, and smaller cities
in the East. The sect in Washington, called the Church of
God and Saints of Christ, was under the leadership of
Bishop H. Z. Plummer who claimed to be the impersona-
tion of Grand-Father Abraham, by which name he was
called within the cult. From Jones's description there
seems to have been little more "Jewish" about it than the
fact that the members commemorated the Passover and
had Sabbath services on Saturday.[15]

The group in Philadelphia, called the Church of God,
under the leadership of Prophet Cherry, exhibits in a
clear-cut form the doctrine that the so-called Negro is
misnamed and that the true Jews are black. In Fauset's
account of the sect, he describes how Cherry will prove
to his congregation that "black folk are not Negroes,
coons, niggers, or shines," and he calls out to "all 'niggers'
to get the hell out of the place!" [16] The ritual and practices
in this church, which the members believe on the basis
of Scripture wrong to call a synagogue, consist of certain

idiosyncratic inventions that the prophet has prescribed on the authority of Scripture. Among these are the fact that he may carry a staff and opens the services by giving six successive beats on a huge drum.[17] Although the members study Hebrew and Cherry keeps a Yiddish and Hebrew Bible on his pulpit, one of my informants—who had moved from Philadelphia to New York in order to join the main sect there—said that Cherry never had any "Temple Worship," that is, a service in Hebrew. It was only in New York that the Negro leaders came in close contact with Jews whose Judaism was based of course not only upon the letter of the Bible but also upon the oral law and the commentary of the Talmudic tradition. It was, indeed, through such contact that these leaders acquired a model for their religion. Harlem at that time was still in large part a neighborhood of Jewish immigrants for whom these leaders undoubtedly worked occasionally as *shabbos goyim* [non-Jews who are employed by orthodox Jews to perform certain minor services for them on the Sabbath, such as turning off lights] or janitors in synagogues.

During the period 1919–1931 there are records of at least eight Black Jewish cults that originated in, Harlem, the leaders of whom were all acquainted and in several cases associated with each other from time to time as congregations would rise, split, collapse, and reorganize. Several of the "rabbis" took "Jewish" names: Mordecai Herman, Ishi Kaufman, Israel ben Yomen, Israel ben Newman, Simon Schurz; and they differentiated themselves from each other in their interpretations or simple knowledge of orthodox Jewish law and custom. A few permitted the eating of pork while most made its prohibition a central commandment. Some acknowledged Jesus as a "Black Jew who was lynched by the Gentiles." Some of the leaders and their followers simply were using their new identity as a basis of getting handouts from Jews. A few were engaged in outright criminal activity. Among these the most famous was Elder Robinson, who ran a "baby farm" in New Jersey, and who was subsequently imprisoned for violation of the Mann Act. As today's leader of Harlem's Black Jews put it, "It sure took a long time to live that one down."

Perhaps the most interesting and important of all these early figures was a man named Arnold Ford, whose origins and ultimate destiny are shrouded in the usual obscurity that attends new prophets. The testimony of those who knew him personally is that he was a man of unusual intelligence. It is certain that he studied Hebrew with some immigrant teacher and was a key link in transmitting whatever approximations there are to Talmudic Judaism in the practices of these sects. Like many of the Black Jews, he was attracted to the "Back to Africa" movement (see Chapter IV, pp. 99-104) of Marcus Garvey which had such a spectacular rise during the early twenties. He was the musical director of Liberty Hall, the headquarters of the Garvey movement in New York. Garveyism did not coincide exactly with his own outlook, for Garvey rejected his counsel to adopt Judaism as the Negro's religion. Nonetheless, in its militancy, its glorification of blackness, its elevation of Africa as the source of all civilization, Garveyism articulated much of what these people were thinking and seeking; and when the Garvey

movement collapsed, the nationalistic impulse beneath
it survived in these religious sects. Legend or hearsay has
it that Ford, tiring of Judaism, emigrated in the early
thirties to Africa where he became a Muslim and where
he subsequently died. As this was in the midst of the
depression and passage money would be rather scarce,
it is equally possible and even more plausible that he
emigrated not to Africa but to Detroit, and that the W.
Fard, Ford, or Farrad who founded the Islamic cult in
that city and Arnold Ford were one and the same.[18] This,
of course, can be only speculative.

In any event, with the disappearance of Ford from the
New York scene, the mantle has fallen and remains to
the present day on the shoulders of Wentworth A. Mat-
thew, who is the vocal and most charming leader of
Harlem's largest Black Jewish congregation. This is the
Commandment Keepers Congregation of the Living God
or, as they often refer to themselves from the name of
their lodge, the Royal Order of Ethiopian Hebrews, the
Sons and Daughters of Culture, Inc. The nucleus of
Matthew's group has been, like Garvey himself, West
Indian. West Indians who had enjoyed greater freedom
and independence tended to look down upon the Southern
Negro, at least until fairly recently, as servile and lacking
in reserve, dignity, and self-control. Whenever Matthew
uses the term "Negro," which he always pronounces in
a derisive manner, or "the colored people in this country,"
as a way of distinguishing themselves from Negroes, he
evokes this regional distinction. The Commandment
Keepers, which has been in existence as an incorporated
group since 1930, had the usual difficulties of making

ends meet during the depression. Since then it was con-
tinuously located on the second floor of a building at
128th Street and Lenox Avenue until 1962, when it moved
to 1 West 123rd Street. There is a branch in Brooklyn,
led by a colleague and disciple; there are several schis-
matic offshoots further down Lenox Avenue.

Apart from the fact that the older people were West
Indians, the group compared with other individuated
sects in Harlem is not very distinctive with regard either
to the socioeconomic characteristics of its members or to
its internal structure. The Black Jews are working people.
Of the women, who constitute between 60 and 70 per
cent of the members who come regularly to services (ap-
proximately 200), the older ones are day workers, the
younger ones work in semiskilled occupations in the com-
merce and light industry in New York. A few of the men
have skilled trades about which Matthew speaks with
pride. As for the structure of the group, it is a tightly-knit
community which is firmly led by Matthew for whom
the members have a great deal of respect and trust.
Although not everyone in the congregation participates
equally in its social and religious life, for those who do
so most intensely, the group is very much the center of
their whole world and there is sufficient activity to war-
rant their coming to the synagogue three or four times a
week. There are several subassociations for charitable and
social work. We shall defer until later a discussion of what
satisfactions the Black Jews get from joining this sect.

Matthew regards himself and is generally regarded as
the leader of Harlem's Black Jews. Considering the rela-
tively small size of the group, which is only about 1000,

Matthew is a well-known figure and has been frequently written about in the Jewish press, the Negro press, and the press in general. The Commandment Keepers is not only the largest Black Jewish sect but also the most interesting—by virtue of the contacts with the Jewish community which they alone have had and their elaborate development of both belief and ritual. Except where otherwise indicated, all of the following remarks about Black Jews refer to the Commandment Keepers.

II

THE WORLD

OF THE

COMMANDMENT KEEPERS

IN THIS CHAPTER we present a sketch of the main thoughts, beliefs, and practices of the Commandment Keepers. Since we want this to be essentially a sketch of the way in which they themselves see their place in the world, we present it with as little commentary as possible.

NEGRO IS THE NAME OF A THING

The Black Jews contend that the so-called Negroes in America are really Ethiopian Hebrews or Falashas who had been stripped of their knowledge of their name and religion during slavery. The term Negro, they further contend, is a word invented by the slavemasters and imposed upon the slaves together with the white man's religion in order to demoralize them; and they did this by instilling in the slaves the view that they had no gods, no ancestors, no principles of right and wrong—nothing worthwhile—of their own.

During slavery they took away our name, language, religion, and science, as these were the only possessions the slaves had, and they were pumped full of Christianity to make them more docile. The word Negro is a badge of slavery which comes from the Spanish word *niger* meaning black thing. Those who identify themselves with Negroes identify themselves with black things, not human beings. Though some say that the word Negro comes from the Niger River, people are named after land, not water. All so-called Negroes are the lost sheep of the House of Israel which can be proved from scripture and they all have birthmarks that identify their tribe. Jacob was a black man because he had smooth skin.*

The corollary of this is that it is impossible for a person who acquiesces in the white man's definition of him as a Negro to have any pride or dignity; for both respect and self-respect depend upon having a "house of your own." The Commandment Keepers thus conceive of themselves as a "lighthouse in a sea of darkness." One of the objects of the Willing Workers Go-Forward Club—a group of women within the sect who perform such social services as visiting the sick, preparing refreshments—is:

To go forward into the highways and hedges, endeavoring to spread the light of the glorious gospel of our God, and also of the truthfulness of the anthropology of the race of people known in the Western Hemisphere as the Negro Race.

An interview with a new member of the sect gives some idea of what it meant for him to have recovered his true name and religion. In answer to the question, "What do you say if someone calls you a Negro?" he replied:

* All such extracts are based on statements or speeches either of Matthew or of the members of the group.

If someone calls me a Negro, I let them know what I am so they will know what they are too. During slavery and darkness they took our name away from us. But all nations have names—Negro is not the name of a nation. If we'd find out about the people that Jesus spoke about, the lost sheep, he meant the House of Israel. When a man is lost and does not know his name, it's like amnesia toward his nationality. I spoke on street corners, wrote a book called "Marks of a Lost Race," explaining the war through scriptures. There were two of us. This buddy went back to his wife, but I couldn't go back to my wife. The spirit got me. Well one night Matthew's name was revealed to me and I came up here. Later on I brought my wife. When I stand before the Torah and hear what God told our fathers and mothers, and what we have lost, it's made me a new person.

If you wouldn't know yourself, you wouldn't prosper. We must follow the Laws of Israel; then we'll have a house of our own and they will recognize us. Just like with your name, if they called you jackass. We should find our name and declare it to the world.

Race prejudice was built up from slavery and in fact there were dark nations which hated Israel too as much as the whites. It's not race prejudice but nation prejudice. God married Israel and said, "I don't want you to bother with these other nations. But through your disobedience, you see what's the result." God married Israel so the other nations were jealous. When Israel will stand up with its own name, others will stop hating us.

Rabbi Matthew is the only man that's got something that benefited our people. I broke up my home to come up here. That's something. Not till we turn back like Rabbi Matthew will our trouble cease. They say we have advanced since slavery, but we are still in back of the whites. But return to one leader and let him point out the way and let him take up the burdens he knows how. The Gentiles elect men to exercise authority over you. But the one who grows up great among you, like Rabbi Matthew, let him be your servant. I feel better since being with Rabbi because I have come back to my customs.

NOT BLACK BUT COMELY

On what basis do the Commandment Keepers conclude
that the so-called Negroes are really the Hebrews of the
Bible? The members of the sect are devoted readers of
the Bible, and know many long passages of it by heart.
What from their own point of view is the scriptural proof
of their identity? There are essentially two main points.
The first is that Jacob was black because he had a smooth
skin "as the black man invariably is," and hence the
patriarchs were black. Solomon was also black, and Matthew contends that the Biblical phrase in The Song of
Solomon 1:5, in which Solomon says, "I am black but
comely, O ye daughters of Jerusalem," should be correctly
translated as black *and* comely. (Indeed, the Hebrew does
permit either alternative.) The second point is that they
are the descendants of the union between King Solomon
and the Queen of Sheba who founded a line of Ethiopian
Hebrew kings from Menelik I down to Haile Selassie, the
Lion of Judah, who is covertly a Hebrew:

Of the three sons of Noah, Shem and Ham were black and
only Japheth, the ancestor of the Gentiles was white. Thus
King Solomon was a black man. After the Queen of Sheba
became his wife in a marriage ceremony taking six months,
she returned to Ethiopia pregnant with the understanding that
the child, if a boy, would be returned to Jerusalem for *bar
mitzvah* [confirmation].* At the age of twelve Menelik, the
son, did come back and remained in Jerusalem until he was
twenty-five. His father, realizing that designs were being made
upon the young prince's life, gave him a company of men with
whom to go to Ethiopia. The priests who accompanied the
young prince deceived Solomon and carried away with them

* All Hebrew-Yiddish terms in both speeches and the narrative
are words actually used by the members of the group.

the original tables of the law instead of the copy which the King had prepared. They are to be found this very day at Axum. Menelik I was the first king of Israel in Ethiopia from whom Haile Selassie—the Lion of Judah—traces his descent in an unbroken line of 613 kings.

Haile Selassie's connection with the Coptic Church is due to diplomatic pressure from Britain which requested in 1896, after the Ethiopian-Italian War, that all kings coming to the Ethiopian throne be Coptic Christians. However, the court at Addis Ababa is closed for business on Friday afternoons and all day Saturday, no *chozzer* [pork] is eaten in his palace, and he follows the Falasha ritual. Haile Selassie is the present King of the House of Israel and this is proof that David should never lack a black man to sit upon the throne of Israel. When Mussolini overran the country, Haile Selassie stopped at Jerusalem to pray in Hebrew before proceeding to the League of Nations. It is from Addis Ababa that I derive my authority as head of the Black Jews in the United States. We are Africans or Ethiopian Hebrews.

A third point, which obviously goes beyond the question of mere identity, is Matthew's insistence that Noah, in Genesis 9:25, did not curse Canaan to be a servant of servants because Noah was drunk and God does not use intoxicated people to execute his curses.

THE ANTHROPOLOGY OF THE BLACK JEWS

Matthew has expounded his views on the origins of the Black Jews in a small handbook for members, and these views are now presented in their entirety.

The Anthropology of the Ethiopian Hebrews
and their Relationship to the Fairer Jews

In order to speed along to a quick understanding, I must treat briefly the history of the sons of men, from Adam, of whom it is only necessary to say that when God decided on the necessity of man's existence, He did not choose to make a black man, or a white man: He simply decided to make man—not white nor black—from the dust of the earth, in whom He encased the reproductive power of all colors, all species, all shades of all races and eventual nationalities. From Adam to Noah, there were only two classes of men, known as the sons of God and the sons of men: a Godly and an ungodly group. In other words, a carnal and a spiritual-minded race of the sons of men, both from Adam.

The two classes eventually met in Noah and his wife: Noah was a son of the Godly (a son of God), he chose a wife from the daughters of men (the carnal-minded), and to the time of the flood he had three sons: Shem, Ham, and Japheth. After the flood Ham took the lead. Nimrod, one of his descendants, created the idea of a tower as the landmark of their capital, that if they became lost upon the face of the earth they might have something to look for as a guide, and also as a security against future floods. They called the name of their tower, or city, Babel. Some have said that Babel means confusion, but this is not so; the word means "Coming to God."

As Cush rose in power, Africa, the entire continent, including Egypt, became the center of the world's cultural and religious education, and thus Ham secured for himself and his posterity for all time, a name—Pioneers of the World's Civilization.

After the fall of Cush came Egypt, under Mizri the second son of Ham, into power. He and Shem amalgamated by intermarriage and the Mesopotamians were produced, an interrace between Shem and Ham. After this came Abraham, the son of Tera; he married his sister Sarah, who was the daughter of his father but not of his mother. She was barren to him, but after many years she conceived by aid of a Hamitic god (Priest) and brought forth Isaac who, in turn, married Rebecca, his uncle's daughter. When she also, after many years, conceived, she brought forth twins, one red and hairy all over like a hairy garment, while the other was plain and smooth, as the black man invariably is. The first, the red and hairy one was called Esau; the plain and smooth brother was called Jacob. This same Jacob, by four wives, begot twelve sons.

After twenty years his name was changed from Jacob to Israel, and automatically his sons became the sons of Israel.

They went into Egypt and abode there four hundred and thirty years. They mingled greatly with the Egyptians by inter-marriage, and thus Shem and Ham were merged into one great people. Of those who left Egypt, there were six hundred thousand footmen, twice as many women, three or four times as many of the half-breed and a host of children. All those who had reached maturity before leaving Egypt died in the wildnerness except Joshua and Calen; even Moses, the greatest of all legislators, died there. But before coming out of Egypt Moses had fled to Median in Ethiopia, only to become servant to the Ethiopian Priest whose daughter he eventually married and begot two sons.

Those two boys were as much Ethiopians as it was possible to be because they were created out of the soil and born in the land, as they were Israelites of the Tribe of Levi, the Priest, because Moses their father was of the tribe of Levi and of the household of Israel. They of necessity had to be black because their father was black, and so was their mother. They were the first Ethiopian Hebrews of the Tribe of Levi. They were half Hamitic and half Semitic. I could go on endlessly to prove the direct connection all along the ages of the two greatest peoples that ever lived in the earth, but I must hasten along.

This great admixture of two great people left Egypt, tarried in the wilderness forty years, and finally came into the land of Canaan. Eventually David, son of Jesse of the Tribe of Judah, came to the throne of Israel, and in time his son Solomon succeeded him.

When Solomon came to the throne, his fame spread the world over, and to the Queen of Sheba, whose name was Candace Queen of the South, she being also of the children of Rachel, one of the wives of Jacob. She also came to pay her respects and to make her portion of the kingdom subject to King Solomon. Eventually she became the wife of Solomon, the son that was born to them was Menelik the 1st. The line of the Falashas are counted from Menelik 1st to Menelik the great, who was the uncle of his Imperial Majesty, Haile Se-lassie, the 1st, the Lion of the Tribe of Judah. It is roughly calculated that before the war there were about a million

Falasha Jews in Ethiopia (about a tenth of the population of 13 million); however, since the war they have been greatly reduced, and fear is entertained for their continued existence. In Harlem, N.Y., there are about three thousand adherents to the faith and who, with pride, lay claim to this glorious heritage. At the central Congregation, 1 West 123rd Street, N.Y.C., there are about eight hundred registered. At 434 Franklin Ave., Brooklyn are also a goodly number. In Philadelphia, Media, Pittsburgh and Sharon, Pa., are goodly groups, also at Youngstown and Ferrell, Ohio, Chicago, Ill., Cullen, Va., St. Thomas, V.I., and Jamaica, W.I.

It is claimed by these that they are among the oldest families of the Jewish or Hebraic race upon the face of the earth, and that they are the only ones to retain their king to sit upon the Throne of David and, outside of Palestine, to retain the six point star on their money. Our manner and customs are strictly orthodox; we are strictly Koshered. Our children are taught to speak the Hebrew language and to live in keeping with all the commandments of the Almighty.

I am the only rabbi with credentials from Ethiopia, sanctioned by both the Chief Rabbi of the Falashas and the National Coptic Church of St. Michael. The National Church must sanction the existence of all other religious bodies in Ethiopia, but none are ever barred or hindered. Religious practices are as free in Ethiopia as in the U.S.A. Thus it is time for the two great people to come together and stand for the true doctrine of the oneness of God.

My prayer is that peace may soon come to the earth, and good will to all men, and an eternal victory for Israel, the elect of the Eternal.

CHRISTIANITY, THE RELIGION OF THE GENTILES

The primary grounds on which the Black Jews seem to repudiate Christianity is that it is not their own. Judaism is the ancestral heritage of the Ethiopians, Christianity is the religion of the Gentiles, which in this sect means whites. In theory this might be assumed to result in a feeling of indifference toward Christianity as merely the religion of another nation, and as the members of the sect look most inwardly to their own rituals this might seem to be the case. But the rejection of Christianity, no matter what freedom from preoccupation with it the high point of their rituals may provide, is hardly an indifferent matter for these people; and Matthew's sermons constitute a self-conscious and running attack on Christianity not merely as an erroneous doctrine but also as the religion of a group which is doomed to an apocalyptic destruction:

This is the Gentile age and it is coming to an end as did all other ages. The antediluvian age was ended by a flood. The stone age ended with the fall of Babel. Then there was the medieval age which closed when the Israelites broke away from Egypt. The patriarchal age ended with the fall of the *Beth Hamikdash* [Temple]. God predicted that he would never again destroy the earth by water but by fire, so he has placed the atomic bomb in the hands of the Gentiles who know only how to make machines and instruments of destruction. In this ungodly world which is filled with idolatry, the Gentiles have had their day. The utter destruction which will be wrought by an atomic war in the year 2000 will leave no one on earth, and will usher in the theocratic age—when God will rule and the Children of Israel will return to their country [variously referred to as Ethiopia or Israel].

Judaism is thus not simply "their" religion but the true religion, the religion of a chosen people:

Christianity violates the Ten Commandments, keeps the Sabbath on the wrong day, and is full of idolatry. It was with Israel that God made the covenant and it is Israel who will be resurrected when the Messiah comes. Only Israel has the Cabbalistic Science. We are the elect of Israel.

One woman in the sect, who evidently had some thoughts of her own on the subject, looked not upon Africa or Ethiopia or Israel but rather upon America as the land belonging to the Jews; her rejection of Christianity is most explicitly connected with expectations about a new distribution of ethnic power:

I want to tell you something that I don't think you know. First, we Jews must stick together although I think the Jews are making too much over Israel. Because every continent belongs to a certain race of people. Asia for the Asiatics. Africa for the Africans. Now this is the land for the Jews because who were the first people here? Indians. Look on an Indian-head penny and what will you see? The face of a Jew. Europe belongs to the Gentiles because if you wanted to put a man in jail, wouldn't you put him in a place with little sunlight? I don't consider you white, by the way.

This war won't be over until the Europeans are back in Europe, and this is why there is going to be another war: the atom bomb is the revelation that was prophesied 3335 years ago and will do the trick.

The sun is the most beneficial thing there is, because it gives us food and warmth. You could get a sun tan too if you went down to the beach. We can take the sun. When some English missionaries were up with the Eskimos, they told them that if they didn't become Christians, they would go to hell. They all said that they'd love to go to a place where there was a little heat.

You people are lucky. You haven't been pumped full of Christianity like we were. But even in slavery our Negro spirituals had nothing to do with Jesus. You know, Go Down Moses, Crossing the Jordan.

They say there are only twenty million colored people in this country. That's a lie. There are at least forty million and five million passing as whites.

Intertwined with such doctrinal and apocalyptic reflections is a moral objection to Christianity or, to be more precise, the Christianity with which they are familiar. This is its hallowing of meekness which, as the following remark by Matthew shows, is immediately perceived in a racial context.

If we could get redemption by the sacrifice of one man, it would be a good thing. But a lot of black men were lynched —for that's what happened to Jesus—and they are not martyrs and they should be. But Jesus was not Christian, he was a Jew of the tribe of Judah. And he was black, and I'm glad to say that I was one of the first to settle that. When the Gentiles find out that Jesus was black, they'll drop him as their Lord overnight.

Related to this is the constant contempt and ridicule which Matthew shows for ecstatic religion that consumes itself in other-wordly orientation.

Some people think that with faith they can do anything [then ridiculed ecstatic prayer], that you can jump off a building and not get hurt. That isn't faith. That's faith without knowledge! Sure you can jump off a building. The fall won't hurt you but it's that sudden stop. Some people think that they don't have to learn to read—"de Lawd's spirit will enter him and he'll be able to see"—[again ridiculed religious ecstasy]. We need what kept the Jews alive for 5000 years. This is more than a few precepts or an oily tongue. We need knowledge.

One might ask, however, knowledge of what and for what? As we shall see, this includes Hebrew, the rules of kosher foods, and the Cabbalistic Science of the House of Israel. One might also expect it to include the Law in the most comprehensive sense. But here a slight perplexity arises. The closer they get to the conception of themselves as the bearers of the Law, the closer they get to Deuteronomy 28 with its prophetic injunction that the Children

of Israel, if they disobey the Law, will be re-enslaved and
carried across the sea in ships. Thus, while in one way
this confirms their identity as Hebrews to themselves, it
also shifts the cause of slavery onto the Negro himself.
With a few exceptions this problem tends to be passed
over in silence.

HEBREW IS NOT A LANGUAGE
OF THE STREET

Hebrew, as the Black Jews contend, is the Lord's language, the sacred language spoken by Adam and Eve in
the Garden of Eden, their language which was stolen from
them during slavery. And they hold it in all the awe and
reverence that they would grant to their most sacred possession.

My grandfather, they tell me, was of pure African stock, and
knew about the Hebrew language. But in slavery we had to
take on the language and religion of our masters. But as
Jeremiah says, "Can the Ethiopian change his skin? Can the
leopard change his spots?" We are Ethiopians only they give
us an odd name.

I've been here since 1928. I got tired of Christianity, of going
from church to church. Got the spirit it wasn't right. Just found
this by myself because I wanted Hebrew. Like I was reaching
out and discovered this.

Besides, as one of the teachers in the Hebrew school
stated at the commencement exercises, with her finger
pointed to the window, "Hebrew is not a language of the
street."

All the new members immediately learn the words
"Shalom" and *"Shalom Aleichem,"* which they thence-

forth use in greeting each other, and begin to study Hebrew in evening classes. (The children come in the afternoon after school where they are taught by Matthew.) The male members are each given a Hebrew name; when they are sufficiently advanced they can be then called to the altar to read a portion of the *Torah* or to recite the blessing of the *Torah*. While some read the words of the *Torah* very haltingly, others read with greater ease. Everyone, of course, knows the blessing, which is soon learned by rote; and some of the Hebrew songs are transliterated.

STRICTLY KOSHER

The Black Jews proudly assert that they are strictly kosher. They use kosher salt and kosher soap and there is no question that apart from Hebrew, the most important single meaningful religious element for these people is observance of the rule against eating of unkosher foods. In this sect these are pork, crabs, catfish, and lobsters as well as duck, frankfurters, and bear. All of these are regarded as unhealthy.

We are the healthiest congregation on Manhattan Island, because we don't eat pork. I didn't need to get vaccinated for smallpox because there isn't any pork in my blood. Of course, some of you have been here only a few years and still have a lot of pork in your system. Also, the reason we don't have evil thoughts is because we eat clean food.

One member said that she used to love bacon but today cannot even stand the smell of it, although another, as Matthew told the congregation with great amusement, did not realize for three years after joining that bacon is pork. Matthew has obviously been questioned by Jews about his inclusion of duck on this list, which is perfectly acceptable to orthodox Jews. His answer was that the swan is unclean and the duck is a member of the same family.

The kosher rules are in a major respect part of an extraordinary preoccupation with disease, physical and mental. Matthew's lectures on Cabbalistic Science are, as we shall see, heavily focused on the problem of going mad in the middle of the night. And in general the subject of health is one to which he frequently turns in the most varied contexts.

Sometimes a little thing can get the best of you. The tuberculosis bacillus enters your nose, infects your trachea, lobes, lungs, transverse colon, kidneys. First you have a cold, then bronchitis, then chronic bronchitis, then you start coughing at all hours of the night, then start spitting blood. We might discuss the gonococcus germ. You know there was a time when you couldn't discuss these things openly.

The woman who, apart from Matthew, is the chief teacher, in telling me how she got into the organization, stated:

I was sick for nearly a year because I kept an ice bag on my face for such a long time that I froze my face. The doctor told me to keep it on for two hours at a time and I even slept with it. I was practically blind in one eye, but the rabbi went down to the drug store and got something and washed my eye out with it, and I can see much better now. I was very sick for nearly a year, didn't get out of that bed for eight months. But the students came up here and took their lessons from me right in my room.

All in all, the importance which the kosher rules have for these people and the very great self-consciousness they have about their diet stems from the conviction that all their life they had been eating poison, imposed on them both by the ignorance of what is a proper diet and by their poverty. Obviously, some of the items they taboo are scavenger foods.

THE CABBALISTIC SCIENCE OF THE HOUSE OF ISRAEL

On Monday evenings the group is constituted as the Ethiopian Hebrew Rabbinical College and Matthew lectures on a variety of subjects. His choice of topic is in fact somewhat informal, but he did outline the following curriculum:

CURRICULUM

Curriculum of the Ethiopian Hebrew Rabbinical College of the Royal Order of Ethiopian Hebrews and the Commandment Keepers Congregation of the Living God, Inc.

First-year Course for all Field Workers, including Revivalists, Daughters of Israel, Prophets and Exhorters:

1. The twelve principles of the doctrines of the cultural house of Israel.
2. Elementary Hebrew.
3. Bible poetry (The Psalms).
4. Prophecies and their allusion to the kingdom to come.
5. Harmony of the Prophecies of the four great prophets: namely, Isaiah, Jeremiah, Ezekiel, and Daniel.
6. Ministerial decorum.
7. Cultural and domestic aid—Grammar.

The Advanced Course

1. Study of the chomesh (The five books of Moses).
2. Lyrics.
3. Advanced decorum and manner of speech in mixed congregations.
4. Ethical presentation of Jewish history.
5. Geography and topography of the holy land.
6. Chronology of sacred writings.
7. The names and characteristics of the congregations of God.
8. Etiquette.
9. Theocracy.
10. Natural history of sacred writings.

This is divided into four terms, comprising two years.

Special Shepherd and Teacher's Course

1. The study of the Mishnah.
2. The apocrypha.
3. Jewish ancient history.
4. Hebraic ancient history.
5. The entire works of Josephus.
6. The Israelites and their related people.
7. Israelitish ancient and medieval history.
8. Topography of the countries connected with sacred writings.

Final Term

1. Jewish months and their scriptural proofs.
2. Talmudic Legalism.
3. Clerical Legalism.
4. Etiquette in general principles.
5. Parliamentary rules.
6. Levitical Priesthood and Temple worship.
7. Special Talmud Torah information.

8. Elementary Greek, Latin, French, Advanced Hebrew, and Sociology.
9. Certificates are given to those who complete the course.

An efficient and able staff of teachers is maintained at all times to accommodate all students.

Members study for many years. Each year there is an annual commencement exercise and qualified students are awarded the degrees of B.D., D.D., and M.H.D. (Master of Hebrew Doctrine). This is one of the most festive ceremonies of the group. Many of the members wear their caps and gowns, which they own. There are speeches by Matthew (who on this evening is addressed not as Rabbi but as Dean), the faculty, and the leading students. This is followed by entertainment and refreshments.

During the period I was with the group, Matthew's lectures to the students of the Rabbinical College dealt principally with the Cabbalistic Science of the House of Israel. Some extracts from these lectures are as follows:

Years ago I gave a complete course in cabbalistic science. I am a doctor of metaphysics and studied mental telepathy. I can tell your thoughts. It took seven years to complete the course: learned how to stop rain, heal the sick. I was in Charlottesville, Virginia, and I said, "I hear a voice speaking to me right now." Then I said, "Mother Johnson, please go see Mother Hubbard right now." When I got back to New York I saw Mother Johnson who said, "I was working on my laundry when I heard the rabbi's voice to go see Mother Hubbard and it was a good thing I went because she was in trouble." Is that conjuring? Is that sorcery?

Conjure, by the way, is a good word. Means compel. Here, I take this match and strike it and compel it to light. The Negroes call it *cunjur*, the whites call it *conjoor*. The atomic bomb is a matter of conjuring, and so are all the forces. The word isn't so bad. But the poor Negro from Africa was made afraid by the Gentile master. That was the only secret he had and the Gentile taught him to be afraid of "spirits."

Cabbalistic science is one of the branches of mental telepathy. Those who thought it conjuring had a dark cell in their minds. This is an angelic science—has nothing to do with rabbit's foot, spiritualism, which is a miscarriage of a spiritual thing, or conjuring spirits out of a graveyard. Lucifer fell into a world of darkness and that's the world the spiritualists penetrate. They set you against your best friends, lead you into the numbers racket. Use dirt and filth: dead man's finger, grave dirt. Cabbalistic things are parchment. The science of Israel is a big thing. It's why we use *talesim* [prayer shawls], candles, and incense. The Catholics faintly imitate us. After this course, you can go out anywhere and make good.

Now I want you to take this down in your notebooks. The angelic world of cabbalistic science is based primarily on twelve foundations and seven elements of spirit. The twelve foundations are heavens: open heaven, the heaven of light, the heaven of darkness, the starry heaven, the heavens of the sun and moon, the angelic heaven (consisting of fallen angels and holy angels), third dimension heaven, the heaven of the throne of God, the heaven of myriads, the heaven of the hard or solid, the soft or liquid, and the gaseous. The seven spirits are wind, water, fire, life or energy, light, power or force, mind or intelligence.

As Matthew then expounded, Cabbalistic Science is a set of secret Hebrew formulae, unknown to the Gentiles, by means of which one can achieve the following: cure rheumatic, restore sight, bring back life to dead babies, keep oneself from going crazy in the middle of the night, change the bad minds of people to good and turn enemies into friends. This is performed through the help of four angels who work in three-hour shifts around the clock: nine to twelve, twelve to three, and so on. In order to get a response from the right angel one has to call his name in Hebrew during the time in which he is on his shift.

There are four cardinal angles to the universe and four angels which are the centers of attraction, and were given names by men, not carnal men, but spiritual men, men who had prayed. The four angels are Gavreel, Michael, Owreel, and Rafarel. The Gentiles mispronounce these names, of course, call them Gabriel, Michael, Uriel, and Rafael [ridiculed this by derisive laughter]. If you don't call them correctly, they won't work. Now how do they work?

Gavreel is the God of darkness and is ours. He works from six to nine, night and day. Now your outer skin is dark but your inner skin is light as you can plainly see if you cut yourself. Gavreel brings harmony. If you're sick and ailing, call upon Gavreel. You must get an answer because angels work with that that is present. A person uttering the name Gavreel seven times in an hour is bound to quiet the nerves because the word Gavreel means harmony. So you are bound to calm yourself even if you're going crazy. Inscribe it on ivory or metal or on parchment with a clean pen and you can't be part of the world. If you want harmony begin prayer and consecration from six to nine. Approach God in the name of *el yoim* [the day] or *el laila* [the night] through Gavreel. You have to know what to say. Words take on bodies. When God spoke, the sun stopped. Your life and health depend on the moon. She's the feminine side of life. Start your business on the new moon, so it can grow with the moon. You wouldn't want to start anything in the fourth quarter when the moon is declining?

At nine o'clock the angels change shifts and Michael comes on. He protects and defends. I prayed daily for our fifty-nine boys in the Army and Navy and they all came back.

At twelve o'clock Owreel goes on. From twelve to three is the time when you really get sick and disease is rampant. If you live through three o'clock you'll probably live through the next day. Call upon Owreel to destroy evil. Owreel has control of all metallic substances, also wood and stone, the atomic bomb, everything that man has put together, trains and cars. Owreel destroys evil, tears it down. Goes before you. Changes the bad minds of people to good. Makes enemies your friends. Binds the bacteriological forces that work against you. Owreel

destroys the power of evil diseases, evil thoughts, the force of
a sharp or blunt instrument. Inscribe his name on any metal.
He will work for you better than voodoo. Israel came out on
top all through the ages because our men knew how to call
God. Do you think the three Hebrew boys who went into the
fiery furnace went in saying "Lawdy Jesus" [here mimicked a
Southern Negro]? They went into the furnace anointed with
the oil of life, which we can't take up tonight, and they tell
me that when they came out they didn't even smell of smoke.
Do you think Daniel cried, "Lawdy Jesus, save me," when he
was thrown to the lions?

Rafarel is the physician. He works from three to six. Call
upon him to give you healing. I have given sight. Sister G——
was nearly blind. I told her one of these days I'm going to
give you sight. Well one day when I felt in the right mood,
I went over to her house in Jersey, washed my hands, poured
my blood into both eyes, and in less than fifteen days she
could walk around by herself. We asked her, "Can you see?"
She said, "A little dark but I can see." Then along came the
evil spirit, a Mrs. S——, and she and Mr. G—— arranged to
have her put in the hospital. They operated and when they
took off the bandages, they marked on her record STONE BLIND!
That's the result of interfering with the work of God.

To cure rheumatic, utter Rafarel over a jar of honey. But
be it known, nobody here has faith in sorcery, superstition, and
witchcraft. If people are crazy, we pray them out. We live on
earth and we try in our religious devotion to make instant
contact with the invisible world around us.

NO NIGGERITIONS

Many journalists who have written about the Black
Jews have commented upon the "Amens," "Halleluiahs,"
and handclapping interspersed throughout the service,
concluding from these that this was "ordinary Negro worship." In addition, one writer had quoted Matthew as
saying, "We are in de House of de Lawd." All this in-
furiates Matthew, and justly so. In the first place, his

pronunciation of English is standard, and whatever dialect there is in the group is not Southern but West Indian. And dialect or no, the ordinary speech of the older members is practically the language of the King James Bible. In the second place, although some expression of enthusiasm is permitted, what is so markedly characteristic of their worship (which a contrast with a Holiness service would immediately make clear), is its restraint and sobriety. There is no swooning, shrieking, screaming, running up and down the room in a state of "possession"— all of which Matthew regards as "niggeritions." A female visitor to the service, as I once saw, began to indulge in emotional shrieks but was cut off abruptly when all the members turned around to stare. As will be recalled from Matthew's lecture on Cabbalistic Science, a most important dimension of Matthew's attack on Christianity consists of a ridicule of the language and gestures of a Southern country Negro in the act of religious ecstasy which he constantly mimics with superb skill to the delight of his flock. Whatever enthusiasm there is in the sect is the preserve of the women. At one high point in the service all the men walk around the synagogue a number of times, led by Matthew who is carrying a Torah, while the women sing a hymn (usually "Round the Walls of Jericho Here We Come"). When the men are called to the Torah, they manifest complete reserve and dignity. The service on the whole is ordered and punctual.

WE CELEBRATE ALL JEWISH HOLIDAYS

The Black Jews have their weekly services on Friday nights and Saturdays, both morning and afternoon, and,

as stated in a poster outside the synagogue, they celebrate
all Jewish holidays, if somewhat in their own way. This
is in addition to such festivities as *bar-mitzvahs* [con-
firmations] and weddings. The Saturday morning service,
which I shall describe briefly, begins about 10:30. There
is a *mezuzah* [miniature scroll] over the door to the
synagogue, which each member touches with his hand
and then kisses as he enters. The men, who sit in the
front, all wear *yarmulkes* [skull caps], and some have
beards. The women, who sit behind the men, wear a
blue and white or solid white uniform with a headdress;
the Revivalists and Mothers have the Hebrew letters for
Zion embroidered on their headdresses. The service begins with a hymn sung by the adult choir. Then everyone
rises, the men put on their *talesim* [prayer shawls], and
all sing the prayer *Shema* [Hear O Israel]. The rabbi an-
nounces the page of *Phillips's Prayer Book* on which the
service begins, although most of the members know.
The rabbi reads along, alternating between Hebrew and
English of the bilingual text, up to the point where it is
indicated that the scroll is to be removed from the ark.
At this time, members who wish to do so "pledge contributions to *Torah*" (a dollar) for the purchase of a new
scroll. Then the rabbi removes the scroll from the ark,
takes the covering off and drapes it over a qualified shep-
herd boy (one of the youngest), blesses the *Torah,* and
the heart of the ceremony commences.

The men file up one at a time to the altar to recite the
blessing of the *Torah.* The rabbi asks each in turn in
Hebrew, "What is your name?" Each replies, also in Hebrew, my name is A, son of B, tribe of (one of the twelve),

son of Isaac, son of Jacob, son of Abraham, son of Terah. Then each recites the blessing and departs from the pulpit. After this, two readers recite respectively in Hebrew Exodus 19 and 20 (the Ten Commandments) from the *Torah*, after which all rise and recite the blessing again. The men march around the synagogue three times, the number three variously explained by the rabbi as standing for past, present, and future, or Abraham, Isaac, and Jacob. The rabbi, carrying the *Torah*, heads the line while the congregation sings "Trusting in the Lord" or a song about the Children of Israel on their route out of Egypt, of which a few lines are:

> So the sign of the fire by night,
> And the sign of the cloud by day;
> Hov'ring o'er, just before
> As they journey on their way.
>
> Shall a guide and a leader be,
> Till the wil-der-ness be past;
> For the Lord our God in His own good time
> Shall lead us to the light at last.

After the singing of a few other hymns, the service is brought to a close with the *Kaddish* [which is the Mourner's Prayer], which the entire congregation stands up to recite, the singing of the Hebrew hymn *Adon Olam*, in the musical version used by Reformed Jews, and a ceremony called dismissal. This is said in Hebrew by Matthew on the Sabbath, by others on week nights, while all stand with bowed heads and both hands raised and clap once at its conclusion.

The afternoon service, which resumes after lunch, is similar except that a different set of hymns is sung and in addition there is a sermon of up to an hour's length, testimonials from the members on the importance of the sermon, and the tithing service which is the collection of the week's dues. After the dismissal Matthew wishes all "*Gut Woch*" (a good week), and the group disperses slowly.

The high point of the year is the Passover festival and the following may make it clear why this is so:

Harlem's Orthodox Jews, the Commandment Keepers, who are celebrating Passover at their synagogue, were told by Rabbi Wentworth Arthur Matthew that he had found much food for thought in comparing the exodus of the Israelites from Egypt with the liberation of Negro slaves in this country.

He said it was "the purpose of God to free the Israelites so that they could give the world the foundation for all good government through the efficiency of the Torah." He added, "So one day the despised so-called Negro will again rise in power through righteousness." [1]

Passover is the occasion for the grandest festivity of the group. The Brooklyn branch joins with the main Harlem congregation to celebrate the *Seder* [Passover meal] on the first night, and during the rest of Passover week— which is celebrated as love week—the synagogue is overflowing with visiting friends. The first night begins as a prayer service; at the conclusion of the one which I observed Matthew stated:

Five thousand seven hundred and seven years ago our forefathers were delivered from slavery. This is the week when the master and the servant both are equals and the master recognizes the servant as a fellow human being, knowing that in reality there is one master above all. If some have a little more than others, that is a privilege of God.

At eleven o'clock Matthew summoned the elders to sit around the *seder* table, set up as a high table in front of the congregation, and he announced that no one who was not circumcised would be allowed to sit in the front row. He then passed out *Haggadahs* [the narrative of Passover] to those seated around the table. The table was covered with ritual foods: horseradish, wine, *matzohs* [unleavened bread], a mixture of liver and wine, hard boiled eggs, scallions, salt water, and lamb. It was a handsome sight and everyone in the audience craned his neck to look as a newspaper photographer took a picture of it.

After reading the blessing over wine from the *Haggadah,* Matthew then instructed one of the little boys to ask, "Why is this night different from all other nights?" Matthew then told him that on all other nights we may eat leavened or unleavened bread but on this night only unleavened bread; on all other nights we may eat any species of herbs but on this night bitter herbs; on all other nights we do not dip even once, but on this night twice; on all other nights we eat and drink either sitting or leaning but on this night we all lean. Matthew then cut up the horseradish into small pieces and distributed it among the congregation, urging everyone to partake. "It will purify the body." Since it was very strong, the group sneezed, choked, and teared to the thorough amusement of all. Matthew then put the *matzohs* into a pillow, broke one; and those in the first row reached into the pillow for the broken one. Brother D——, who got it, thereby became a favorite son. He sat down at the *seder* table and Matthew told him what a blessing it was, pointing to

the other favorite sons seated around the table. Then he
leaned on Matthew's arm and the latter said a blessing
over him. After finishing, Matthew said, "I know one of
you will betray me." Matthew called for lamb and invited
Brother D—— to have some. Inadvertently they both put
their hands in the bowl at the same time. The congregation at once stood up and the situation was filled with
tension while Matthew asked God to nullify this action.
Then dinner was served—consisting of lamb, *matzohs,*
and wine, which had been prepared by the Willing
Workers, who also distributed the plates of food.

After dinner, visiting clergymen were invited to address the congregation and the evening ended at a fairly
late hour. During the rest of the week there is some religious service every night, but nothing quite so elaborate
as the *Seder.*

The religious beliefs of the sect were codified by Matthew as "The Twelve Principles of the House of Israel":

THE TWELVE PRINCIPLES OF THE DOCTRINES OF ISRAEL
WITH SCRIPTURAL PROOF

Principle No. 1. *The New Creation.*—Gen. 1:1, 5; Ez. 14:6;
    Isa. 28:11, 12; Ez. 36:26, 28; Ez. 14:26, 31; Jer. 31:31; Joel
    2:28-39; Mal. 1:2

Principle No. 2. *The Observance of All the Laws of God,
    Given to Us Through Moses Our Teacher.*—Gen. 2:1, 3;
    Ex. 31:18, 32, 15, 16; Deut. 29:29; Isa. 58:13, 14; Dan.
    7:25; Ez. 8:16; Num. 15:32, 33; Psalm 1:1, 4; Ez. 46:1

Principle No. 3. *Divine Healing.*—Ex. 23:25; Ex. 15:26; Psalm
    103:1, 3; Isa. 53:4, 5; Psalm 41:2, 4; Jer. 8:22; 2 Chron.
    30:20; Psalm 107:20; Hos. 7:1

Principle No. 4. *The Administration of Feet Washing and All
    the Rites of the Passover.*—Gen. 18:3; Gen. 19:2; 43:24;
    34:32

Principle No. 5. *Tithes and Offerings; the Early Duty of the People of God.*—Gen. 14:18, 20; 28:20, 22; Lev. 27:30, 32; Mal. 3:8, 12; Neh. 10:37, 39; Deut. 14:21; Hag. 1:1, 6

Principle No. 6. *The Eating of Koshered Foods According to Israel's Law.*—Lev. 11:1, 12; Deut. 14:2, 3; Isa. 65:4-5; 66:17

Principle No. 7. *Everlasting Life.*—Gen. 5:24; 2 Kings 2:11; Hos. 13:13, 14; Psalm 49:6, 9; 118:17; Prov. 7:1, 3, 23; 6:23

Principle No. 8. *Absolute Holiness According to the Law of God.*—Gen. 17:1; Exod. 3:5; Deut. 14:2; Ex. 19:6; Lev. 10:10; 20:7; Psalm 86:2; Isaiah 6:3; 35:8

Principle No. 9. *The Resurrection of the Dead (Black Israel).* —Hos. 13:13, 14; Ezra 37:11, 12; Job 14:5-14, 15; 19:26; Isaiah 35:10; Ezek. 37

Principle No. 10. *The Restoration of Israel.*—Isa. 1:26; Jer. 30:17, 18; 27:22; Joel 2:25; Isa. 11:10, 11, 12; Jer. 31:31, 34

Principle No. 11. *The Coming of the Messiah.*—Deut. 18:15, 18, 19; Mal. 3:1; Isa. 41:2, 3, 4; Isa. 9:6, 7

Principle No. 12. *The Theocratic Age.*—Gen. 49:9-10; Isa. 11:1; 5:9-10

(Selected by Rabbi W. A. Matthew, first in all the world to select these twelve keys to a systematic study of the Holy Scriptures, because he had the welfare of his people at heart.)

FATHERS AND SONS

When Matthew uses the term Negro to refer to other black men—which he generally pronounces in a contemptuous way as "Nee-gro"—he is referring for the most part either to what may be called a Sambo in the act of religious frenzy or to a stereotype of a lazy, ignorant, "mean" Negro. As my acquaintance with the group progressed, it became clear that their repudiation of crime, delinquency, and shiftlessness was in every way as important to them as the knowledge of their name.

People learn Negro habits. We have to emphasize a certain aloofness. This gives us dignity and self-respect, which makes us an example. The kids, for example, play with Negroes. But I tell them, "Keep your things tidy in school. Apologize quickly if something goes wrong and don't talk back to your teacher. Don't act up like Negroes." Among the Negroes there were conscientious objectors and other crazy things.

It is the proudest boast of the Commandment Keepers that the group is completely free of crime or juvenile delinquency. The children are in the Hebrew school in the afternoons where they are taught by Matthew, and although he is very affectionate toward them, he nonetheless demands and gets respect from them. Furthermore, at least half of his sermons, to take a rough estimate, are concerned with delinquency and have the intention of supporting authority, particularly paternal, in the family:

I will take for my text Proverbs 13:24. "If the child has a rebellious spirit, drive it out with a rod." And in olden times, if the child was unmanageable, the council had the power to use a strap on him and give him as much as forty stripes. . . . I read in the paper about a Negro policewoman taking a white woman to jail. Usually it's the other way around. But this is a little different. The mother and father weren't living together and she was getting twenty dollars a week for support which she was spending on herself, and not taking care of the boy. The father wanted to take care of him, but she didn't want to give up her twenty dollars a week. The child became wild and they arrested the mother. That's the way it should be. Children must be punished, but it's not always necessary to use a strap. Ask my two sons. I never laid a hand on them during their whole development. You have to have patience. It's not always the children's fault. Some mothers just don't know how to take care of their children. They'll call "Johnny," ha, ha [parodying an ineffectual woman whining], "come to the table," once, twice, instead of "WHY DIDN'T YOU ANSWER WHEN YOU WERE

CALLED; AND HAVING HEARD, WHY DIDN'T YOU COME!" And there are some parents who always take the side of the child against the teacher. No wonder they learn to disobey. If you can't handle your children, give them to me. And there won't be any marks on them either. I'm a juvenile officer of this precinct, and if I can't handle them, I'll take them to the police station. One policeman told me that there's more law on the end of his night stick than in all the books. People are always complaining about the policeman, but he has a wife and children too. The worst thing that can happen is that when you are out, someone comes into your house and destroys your furniture or mugs you, puts a bullet through your head. Or when you're in your house you hear a knocking on the door: MATTHEW, COME ON TO THE STATION. YOUR SON'S WANTED FOR MURDER. Better the child should be dead right now.

You children don't have to play with the riff raff on the street. People will say that I'm not democratic. Well, democracy doesn't mean that you have to have criminals for friends. THERE ARE CULTURAL DIFFERENCES.

I was walking down the street and grabbed a boy who was standing on the curb, would have been killed by a car, and he swung at me. That's gratitude. Look around when somebody grabs you—you may lose YOUR ARM, YOUR LEG, OR YOUR LIFE. If a child did that to me, I'd shake him up properly.

The exhortation in behalf of what one may call old-fashioned morality goes hand in hand with the ascetic or temperate standards of personal behavior upheld by the group. These acquire fortification from the fact that the atmosphere of the sect in an over-all way stands for self-restraint. Their entire religious worship, in the emphasis it gives to ritual as opposed to the expression of enthusiasm, in the first instance constitutes a discipline for these people and, as has been said above, is self-consciously contrasted by them with the abandon that they identify as the hall mark of lower-class Negro religion. The self-imposition of food taboos are equally a restraint. And, to turn to habits of deportment, there is great sobriety in dress. Matthew and the older men dress almost entirely in black. It was interesting to notice among the new recruits the gradual disappearance of flamboyant and highly colored clothing, and the large-brimmed hats for men that are so common in Harlem. And all this is done without a word being said, for there is no explicit rule about it. The Black Jews abstain from whiskey but sherry is permitted. Although nothing was ever said about smoking, I never saw anyone indulge in it.

JEWS IN BABYLON

The Black Jews, in contrast with the Muslims, are too small in number to sustain the kinds of communal enterprises that the latter have built up, such as restaurants. Regardless of size, the Black Jews are uninterested in that kind of radical withdrawal from the outside world which has induced the Muslims to form private elementary schools. The educational institutions of Black Jews, which have broadly similar aims, are supplementary to the public schools, achievement in which is esteemed. Matthew, furthermore, values the few contacts he has had with Jewish educational and religious institutions where he has from time to time been invited to speak. There is, of course, a great deal of informal cooperation in the group. For years Matthew would transmit requests telephoned to him for domestic help to the women in the group. The one cooperative project that is so characteristic of the group is the settlement in suburban Babylon, L.I., which so many of them have their hearts set on. As one member put it:

If the colored people would get some land somewhere and build up nice homes and have a center where the women can come up and do good housekeeping, it will show the lower class the way. You can't do anything in the slums. Here in the U.S. when the white people get tired of a house, they move out in the country and sell the old house to colored. The colored man has to take out a mortgage and keep paying for repairs. It keeps him down. The only way is for a group to build new homes for the colored people and put the people who know how to use them in there, but who will not high hat the others and teach the other persons how to appreciate them. There's nobody to tell them that.

Through its incorporated lodge, the Royal Order, the group bought a tract of land, plots of which are then resold to individual members for the erection of single family dwellings. At first, they experienced a small amount of vandalism. The windows in one of the houses were broken. But police protection stopped this. Matthew places great value on this project as a way of getting the children out of the slums.

III

THE BLACK JEWS

AND THEIR

FAIRER BRETHREN

THE IMPULSE that generated and sustains this sect is the members' belief that the so-called Negroes are the descendants of the tribes of Israel. For this conviction they are no more dependent upon contact with Jews than were the Judaistic English Puritans in the seventeenth century or than are the Negro Muslims, in a parallel way, with orthodox Muslims. Nonetheless, Jews in the New York area, from the first days of these sects to the present day have had a strong interest in, if not fascination for, what is from their point of view so manifestly an oddity. At least a dozen Jewish visitors, always courteously received, come to the services each Saturday morning. A row of chairs is reserved for them, they are invited to recite the blessing and, if they wish, to address the congregation or to ask questions about the practices and beliefs of the Ethiopian Hebrews. Matthew in turn has been invited to lecture before Jewish organizations in the metropolitan area. Fleeting and even impersonal as these contacts have been, they have had a significant effect upon the life of this sect, for they have provided an entree for observing and getting information about Jewish life. As a result, the Black Jews have been able to fashion a ritual which, notwithstanding all that it preserves of their former experience, nonetheless approximates much more the orthodox model than does that of the Black Muslims (who have dispensed with virtually any ritual). For a Negro to tell a Jew that he too is really a Jew puts him in a position where no matter how fantastic his claim may seem he is taken seriously and wondered at. The natural response of a Jew is to try to figure out how they became Jews in the first place. As may be readily imagined, there has been much speculation in an attempt to account for them on the basis either of descent or of some regularized conversion. One theory, for example, somewhat suggested by the fact that so many of them were from the West Indies, is that they were descendants of slaves of Sephardic Jewish slaveholders in the West Indies (who, in fact, did not Judaize their slaves). By far the most important of these external speculations in its effect on the sect was the idea that they might be Falashas. These are in fact people living in Ethiopia practicing a peculiar if not primitive form of Judaism. They have no knowledge either of Hebrew (they use Ge'ez, as do their Christian compatriots, as the language of their prayers), or of the oral Law. Their prescriptions are drawn entirely from the Pentateuch. They practice circumcision, observe the Sabbath with strictness, and observe the commandments regarding ritual cleanness; but then too so do many other Ethiopians whose Christianity, which is highly syncretistic, retains many Judaic elements. The Falashas know nothing of the postexilic history and celebrate none of the postexilic Jewish feasts.[1] For many years it was thought that they were Hebrews who after the first exile became separated in their southward migration from the main body of Jews and from whom they remained permanently cut off.[2] Ullendorf questions this and it may be of some interest to quote his scholarly judgment in detail:

The present writer feels convinced that all the evidence available points to the conclusion that the Falashas are descendants of those elements in the Aksumite Kingdom who resisted conversion to Christianity. In that case their so-called Judaism is merely the reflection of those Hebraic and Judaic practices and beliefs which were implanted on parts of southwest Arabia in the first post-Christian centuries and subsequently brought into Abyssinia. If this opinion is correct, then the religious pattern of the Falashas—even though it will have undergone some change in the past 1,600 years—may well mirror to a considerable extent the religious syncretism of the pre-Christian Aksumite Kingdom. It is in their living testimony to the Judaized civilization of the south Arabian immigrants and their well-nigh complete cultural ascendancy over the Cushitic and other strata of the original African population of Ethiopia that we must seek the value and great interest of the Falashas today—and not in their rehabilitation as a long lost tribe of Israel (which is historically quite unwarranted). Like their Christian fellow-Ethiopians, the Falashas are stubborn adherents to fossilized Hebraic-Jewish beliefs, practices, and customs which were transplanted from South Arabia into the horn of Africa and which may here be studied in the authentic surroundings and atmosphere of a Semitized country.[3]

In the early twenties (when the Black Jewish sects were forming in New York), by co-incidence, Jews in America and England learned that the Falashas in Ethiopia were experiencing poverty and persecution, and formed an organization, the Pro-Falasha Committee, to give them aid. In the course of its work, the leader of this organization in New York, Dr. Jacques Faitlovich, learned of the existence of a Black Jewish congregation in New York and called on Arnold Ford to find out if they were Falashas. Even though they had already evolved the identity as Ethiopian Hebrews, it is my guess that up to this point they had never heard of the term Falashas—for neither had many other people. Dr. Faitlovich left them with the view that they were "misled." Nonetheless, out of this interchange the very knowledge that there were people in Ethiopia whom the Jewish community recognized as Jews and who were called Falashas immediately became their most treasured insight. It was, so to speak, the "missing link" which for them fundamentally settled the question of their identity in a scientific manner.

As with this, so has it been with other elements of practice and belief. Every question put to them by a Jew of the sort, "Do you do this?" "Do you eat kosher meat?" "Do you people have your own *mohel* [ritual circumcisor]?" "Are you Sephardic?"—questions arising out of the same curiosity that Jews would have about the customs of Jews whom they might meet in foreign lands —has provided information, terms, and rules from which the leaders, who were very eager to learn, gleaned something about what they were supposed to do or be, regardless of the satisfaction that the interrogators had with the answers.

The net result of all this, given this erratic way of acquiring a new religion, is what amazingly looks at first sight to a visitor like a Jewish service. And given the complexity of traditional Judaism, this in itself is something of a feat. But of course Talmudic Judaism not only rests on a core of learning but is also a way of life which even on the level of an unlearned person has to be lived in to be known. The myriad of traditional details which, for example, an ordinary Jewish housewife would know, constitute a world the Black Jews hardly penetrate or could be expected to penetrate. The prohibition against eating pork, as anyone familiar with orthodox Judaism knows, is only the beginning of what it means to be kosher; and the complex of rules about separate dishes for meat and milk foods, let alone a precise understanding of what kosher meat is—and which certainly includes kosher frankfurters—are things that play no role in the sect and which they at best are aware of only vaguely. The social habits of Jews, the way, for example, in which they would spend a Friday night, are things that are obviously outside their experience. Still it was curious to note the way in which certain typically Jewish expressions filtered into the sect. One woman, I recall, before Passover, excused herself from a conversation with the explanation that she had to "prepare for *Yontif* [holiday]." What this preparation could possibly have consisted of, I was never able to figure out—since the members spent not only the *seder* night but practically the rest of the week as well in the synagogue!

But whatever the appearance of the worship may be on first sight, upon prolonged observation the syncretistic character of the religion becomes evident. At work in the Passover *seder*, for example, was a re-enactment of the

drama of the Last Supper, which is not part of the traditional *seder* celebration. But it is the essence of this mode
of "Judaizing" that the Black Jews are unaware of the
syncretism involved. The Ethiopian Hebrews think they
are orthodox Jews and it would be a misunderstanding
of their behavior not to respect the sincerity of this belief.
The one feature of their service where Matthew explicitly
states he deviates from orthodox Jewish practice, since he
has obviously been questioned about this, is the use of
a male and female choir with piano accompaniment,
which he frankly admits they like. One point which makes
the panoply of beliefs and practices so curiously complicated is that Ethiopian Christianity and folklore is itself,
as mentioned above, a Judaic-Christian syncretism.[4] Thus,
odd details that may be gleaned about the practices of
Ethiopians, which include circumcision and the differentiation between clean and unclean animals, in a strange
way "fit" into their pattern of beliefs. And Haile Selassie,
one must remember, is indeed called the Conquering Lion
of the Tribe of Judah.

As for what the Jewish world thinks of this sect, I
would say first that most of the visitors who come to the
services come with good will and if they are somewhat
puzzled by a number of the details, such as being as-
signed a tribe when they come to the *Torah,* they still
leave it in the same spirit in which they came. It must be
recalled that no matter how they may view the service
the phenomenon of Negroes wanting to be Jews cannot
help but make some appeal to Jewish solidarity. Of course,
any number of writers have attacked the sect as outright
frauds; but to look at them in this way seems to me mis-

takenly to pull them much further into the Jewish world
than they really are and loses sight of the racial meaning
of their beliefs. On the other hand, they have had a
number of Jewish champions, some of whom think they
are really Falashas, others who would like to bring them
to genuine Judaism, still others who are just cranks. Many
of the women worked for Jewish families among whom
they enjoyed a very good reputation. Matthew, although
he believes that intermarriage with white Jews would be
unwise given present conditions in America, would like
very much to be granted some kind of official recognition
as the Chief Rabbi of Harlem's "orthodox Jewish community" by a central rabbinical council. In published
statements he has expressed resentment at the fact that
his application for membership in this council has not
been approved. However, some years ago, the Jewish
Education Committee, in reply to his request for financial
assistance, sent a visitor to the Hebrew School and did
offer to take charge of the education of the children provided they be taught by the Committee's teachers. Matthew refused this offer on the grounds that he was teaching "Sephardic" and could not permit "Ashkenazic" influences, though the Committee did send a supply of
books. Whether Jews, individually or collectively, either
could or would wish to go further in accepting, recognizing, or, what is more to the point, assisting the Black
Jews with funds and opportunities is of course an internal
matter where strict standards, in certain contexts, cannot
help but be raised. In general there has never been any
racial barrier raised by the Jewish community to any
Negro who wished to convert to Judaism. One family

actually joined the Institutional Synagogue when it was still functioning in Harlem thirty years ago. But this is the only instance of this sort, at least in New York, that has come to my attention. Obviously, any real demand that they modify their practices would be rejected because it would mean the disintegration of the sect. Given the importance which it has as a community in the lives of its members, any relationship with them would thus have to avoid a collision with their beliefs. Although they cannot simply be bracketed together with other historical exotic Jewish groups, there is an extraordinary openness, particularly on the part of Matthew, to relationships with Jews, and, with all the perplexities of their beliefs, a desire to be a Jew that Jews might wish to take into account, provided one is prepared to blur certain questions. To be sure, membership on a rabbinical council is one thing; and in all fairness to Matthew I believe he was induced to put himself into such an embarrassing position by a white person outside the sect. However, a number of the children are studying Hebrew in the high schools of New York; and it is conceivable that scholarships might be granted to the children to attend Jewish summer camps and that some assistance might be given the congregation toward obtaining or furnishing better quarters. These gestures need hardly raise any doctrinal issues.

As for what the rank and file think about Jews, they are on the one hand Jews and on the other hand whites and this brings about, to say the least, a strange ambiguity. For what it is worth, I asked members whether they felt closer to white Jews than to white Gentiles. Here are some typical replies:

I do not know. I have to prefer white Jews because they belong to me. The Gentiles, I don't know [shrug]. But I prefer to have dealings with white Jews. I went to the chicken market the other day and said something in Hebrew and Bernie laughed. And I said, "Bernie, you don't know what I said." Then I said something in Yiddish and German. I can just speak a little you know.

Yes. They're naturally closer to me. They were entrusted with the Law before it came to us, not the Gentiles. I know plenty of white Jews. But some Gentiles are very nice. I worked for a family out on Long Island before I came here, and I raised their boy since he was a baby. They're Southern folk and they're used to black people, you know. Always had them around to do the servant work. Well, they were very nice to me. In fact I was privileged to go to his sister's wedding.

One older man said to me:

Ever since they operated on me, my spine and stomach have been giving me trouble. They operated the wrong way. They should have done it up and down but they cut me across. A Gentile doctor did it. There was a Yiddish doctor there who told me it was a bad job. He came over to me one Shabboth, saw me reading my Bible. Well, I don't read the Bible every day, but I told him that I was a Jew and this was my day for reading the Bible. So he told some other doctors, "You see that fellow over there, he's a Jew." He was a good doctor too. [Several weeks later, this man said to me:] Ethiopia would be a big country today if you people [that is, whites] hadn't cut it up.

And occasionally the Black Jews forget that they are Jews when complaining about the fact that "the Jews" own all or most of Harlem!

The obverse of this ambiguity in identification is seen in their relations with Negroes outside the sect. The services are freely open to all visitors. Matthew is very friendly to them, sets them at ease immediately, informing them politely that "we keep our hats on here," and always invites them to return. On one occasion Matthew went out of his way to explain to the Christians in the audience, who are never referred to as Gentiles, that "we are not Negroes. But I have a black skin, I have wide nostrils, thick lips, and when something goes wrong, I say 'Na-a-a' too." During Passover week clergymen of other sects who were old friends and acquaintances of Matthew would visit the services. One was the archbishop of the Black Coptics, who believe that the so-called Negroes are really Hamites. As is customary, he was invited to the pulpit to address the congregation. In the course of his remarks he stated, "And don't forget, we are not Negroes. We are Egyptians." This, on the night when the Children of Israel were celebrating their flight from Pharaoh, was too much even for the usual reserve of the Black Jews.

Many commentators, particularly Jewish ones, who project onto the group their own experiences, have automatically assumed that the Black Jews carry a "double burden" of discrimination—both race and religion. This is simply not true; although they often answer in the affirmative when asked whether they experience "anti-Semitism" too, I am not sure they really understand what is involved in this question. Far from feeling discriminated against for being Jewish, they feel the pride of having recovered their true heritage. If there is any discriminating vis-à-vis other Negroes, it is *they* who do it; and as far as practical social relations are concerned the Negro world regards them, as one may expect, as another one of the many curious sects which abound in Harlem. To the ques-

tion "Do you have any contacts with colored people outside the group?" two older members replied:

None. They don't speak my language. But I feel friendly to
certain groups. The only way I go anywhere is if they have a
program. They patronize us and we go to theirs.

We are all mixed up here so we can't shun them. But I
belong only to the Royal Order of Ethiopian Hebrews.

A new member, whose reply accurately indicates where
the sect really rests in Negro opinion, answered:

Yes. They kind of scorn at me. They scorn at my sons too.
Make fun of me: "He try to call himself a Jew." But it doesn't
bother me because I know myself. Most of the people I know
are outside the group, but I don't eat in their homes.

But if solidarity with other Negroes seems to be complicated, it at least has an objective basis as contrasted
with their parallel thoughts about Jews. To some degree
fellow-Jewishness, by virtue of its artificiality, is even a
barrier to real trust and friendship with Jews or, perhaps,
conceals the real basis of such friendships where they
arise. My own rapport with the sect did not really develop until I realized that they were far more interested
in outrages committed against Negroes than in any events
within the Jewish world. Nonetheless, as verbal as this
solidarity is, it is not without a sociologically interesting
effect on the fate of the sect. From their strict ideological
position, they would assert that the true Jews are black
and the white Jews are frauds, "the product of intermarriage." This has been voiced by some of the sects. Matthew,
in addition, has responded to his failure to be accredited
by the orthodox Jewish community of New York with the

assertion that the Black Jews are the only really kosher congregation in New York and that 80 per cent of the white Jews are Reformed, eat pork, and have changed their names! On the nights when Jewish visitors are not present there is a good deal of this in addition to general anti-white hostility. Yet, all this notwithstanding, the iota of solidarity which exists among them and Jews, and particularly the desire to be accepted by Jews as legitimate Jews, has blunted and diluted the racialist content of the sect's beliefs. The invitation that has been offered to them, so to speak, by the Jewish world to prove that they are Falashas has put them in a position where they feel compelled, before this external tribunal, either to maintain that they have a provenance different from that of other Negroes or at least to be silent about their real belief, which is that *all* so-called Negroes are really Falashas. The reluctance to face the Jewish world with complete candor in these respects has been the cause of all the misunderstanding about the sect and between the sect and the Jewish world. As for the Negro world, the result of all this is that the Black Jews have signally failed or have been uninterested in developing these beliefs into as militantly an anti-white popular ideology as the Black Muslims have done. The fact that they are much more pious than the most vocal Black Muslims is also a factor in its own right which is not to be disregarded.

Earlier I raised the possibility that the key founder of the Black Muslims in this country was a man who had "graduated" from Black Judaism. If this be the case, he correctly foresaw that Judaism did not offer any real possibilities as the basis of an anti-white racial movement.

The existence of Jews presented insuperable difficulties. Among other things, anti-Jewish sentiment among Negroes is hardly conducive to a mass conviction that they are Jews. Even if this did not exist, the mere presence of Jews in the society, whose claim to be such cannot be really disregarded, poses a tremendous obstacle to the opinion that the true Jews are black. Now orthodox Muslims in this country have denounced the Black Muslims with perhaps greater vigor than any Jew has cared to exert with regard to the Black Jews; and given the notoriety which the Black Muslims have acquired, this is not hard to understand. But it has in no way impeded the growth of the movement. In fact, I doubt whether very many of the members have ever seen an orthodox Muslim. They are not welcome at their services. The result is that the Black Muslims, in propagating the view that the so-called Negroes are really Muslims, have not had the kind of interferences which the Black Jews have had. Still for many years the two sects were for all practical purposes completely parallel. Present in both was the same mythology about a recovery of the ancestral religion which had been stolen from them by the whites which was used to support, in behavior, a firm and steady repudiation of the white man's stereotype of the lower-class Southern Negro's ways, mentality, and habits. If one knew nothing more about these sects than the fact that the Black Muslims abstain from, as harmful foods, cornbread and black-eyed peas, which were the stereotyped staples of the rural Negro's diet, one would have a substantial key as to the aim of these sects. In the past five years, however, the Black Muslims have attracted the leadership of intellectuals who do not seem to be pious people but who see in the movement a political force and talk to the Negro masses in political terms. These leaders, as is perhaps well known today, have raised the anti-white overtones implicit in their rejection of Christianity to a blatant attack on white society not merely or even particularly because of its adherence to a false religion but rather, as they contend, because the country will eventually belong to them. Their militancy, organization, and numbers have given them notoriety and have made whites fear them, which has by no means been distasteful to them. But of equal or even greater interest is their attack on Negro leadership, in demanding social integration, for "pushing themselves where they are not wanted." This attack, as well as those autonomous institutions and activities they have developed—such as schools and restaurants—make it impossible not to see the autoemancipatory impulse which is the fundamental drive behind all these nationalistic sects—Black Muslim, Black Jewish, Black Coptic. We now turn to a discussion of this impulse and its future in Negro society.

VARIETY AND DISSENT

WITHIN

NEGRO LEADERSHIP

NEGRO LEADERSHIP has typically been classified into two polar types of behavior: accommodation and protest. This dichotomy, for example, was a central element in Gunnar Myrdal's analysis of the Negro problem.[1] Accommodation means that, at least in public statements, the leadership accepted or did not challenge the fabric of segregation—on the basis either of prudential considerations of what could be realistically demanded in a given situation for the good of the Negro community or of private contentment with private gains from segregation. The second type of leadership, conversely, took and still takes the form of public attack upon, certainly, the legal basis of segregation but also upon the whole idea of segregation itself. Much of the polemics of this second type of leadership was concerned, as may be expected, with an attack upon the accommodating leadership within the Negro world. Without question this dichotomy "fits" a certain phase of tension and conflict within Negro society. It reflects the way in which the actors, or some of the actors, involved in these internal conflicts might have viewed them. One easily recognizes in the very dichotomy itself the point of view, for example, of those Negro writers and intellectuals who attacked Booker T. Washington for his Atlanta speech of 1895, in which he stated, "In all things which are purely social we can be as separate as the fingers. . . . " The question that arises, however, is how can one fit into this polarity the Garvey Back-to-Africa movement and the nationalist religious sects? To call them accommodating because they pursue and even demand certain features of a separated social life seems to miss the entire point of their militant attack on white society. To call them protest leadership, which they indeed are, is to bracket them together with a point of view within Negro society between which there is mutual opposition. The leaders of the NAACP have not been admirers of the Black Muslims. Such a classification would thus minimize and ultimately obscure the importance of the tension as seen from the point of view of the actors themselves. This suggests that there may be a more comprehensive dimension involved which as a basis of classification corresponds more precisely with what is going on today in Negro thought and opinion. This dimension, I suggest, is that on which a deeper set of tensions and conflicts is to be located. This is a tension between the quest for autonomy—moral, cultural, political—of the American Negro as a people or a community *and* the quest for the right to be integrated as individuals into a multiracial, universalistic society. The fact that a conflict of this sort has been so late in becoming, so to speak, respectable is one of the interesting features of changing American Negro society. With this dimension in mind, we now turn to an examination of the major divisions about policy in Negro opinion.

The one sphere of Negro life which is autonomous, that is, as autonomous as any voluntary institution can be in a political society, is the church. While the Negro church is segregated, in a crucial measure it has been and still is self-segregated or self-selected; it is to this, indeed, that it owes its strength as the integrating institution of Negro society. During slavery, when unsupervised meetings of any kind among slaves were viewed with suspicion, Negroes had to obtain permission to conduct their own services in "their own way." In the North the Negro church owes its origin to a withdrawal from white churches of free Negroes who refused to be segregated in the gallery.[2] From then onward it has offered an easy avenue for leadership, given that tradition of Protestantism which has been most prevalent among Negroes, as well as an over-all sphere of independence which Negroes themselves financed and controlled. To be sure, criticism of segregation has included attacks on the exclusionist practices of white churches. There have been, in the recent past, occasional "kneel-ins." But as far as the Negro masses are concerned this is very much on the surface of things. In the sharpest contrast to segregation in public schools, there would be no support in Negro society for the self-liquidation of the Negro church, no matter how logically the proponents of such a policy might justify it. Charles S. Johnson aptly summarizes the role that this institution had in Negro society:

Blocked off from virtually all other channels of expression, members of this race have found in the church their own outstanding social institution. It has provided a substitute for political organization and has furnished a channel for social as well as religious expression; it has been the center for face-to-face relations, for communication, for recreation, and for physical as well as psychological escape from their troubles. It has been welcomed by Negroes in areas where physical separation in worship was not demanded.[3]

But with the exception of this one sphere, the axis of the main stream of Negro protest and certainly that which is most vocal today has been turned in another direction. Far from being concerned with the preservation of autonomous Negro institutions, this protest has been so focused upon combating legally *imposed* segregation that any proposal to justify self-separation is viewed, first, as abject surrender to the deepest wishes of racist bigots and, second, as a rationalization for advantages which one was privately enjoying behind "the walls of segregation" and which were created by those walls. Such, for example, would be the position of an incompetent Negro functionary in a segregated institution who is protected from having to compete with qualified whites by the existence of segregation.

Akin to this is the position of a Negro who, as the agent of a white, is able to exercise power over other Negroes. Now it is true, on the one hand, that segregation can indeed create vested interests of this sort, although it is

not without significance that no Negro, whatever his
private vested interests, could publicly advocate and defend legal segregation. On the other hand, it is also true,
as such critics of "integrationism" as the Black Muslims
have voiced, that the Negro world is permeated with self-
contempt and feelings of inferiority vis-à-vis whites, and
that it is an indication of the weakness of the Negro's
position, of his lack of self-respect, that he should regard association with whites qua whites as more "prestige
worthy" than association with other Negroes. We shall
take up the issues raised by these polemics in due course.

For the moment it suffices to emphasize that the primary reason why legalist protest has acquired its shape
and direction and has been so indifferent, not to say
antagonistic, to the idea of a voluntary community as a
social goal is that the Negro has had in these respects no
fundamental freedom of choice. The decisive fact in the
history of the Negro in America has been his inequality
in public law. The Negro community has always been a
segregated community. It was not preceded by a voluntary community for the same reason that there was no
voluntary emigration of Negroes to the New World. There
has been thus nothing clear and unambiguous to return
to or to sustain them as a basis for cohesion. Between
this and the massive structure of legal inequalities which
face the Negro, he has not been even remotely in a position to be concerned about his disappearance as a people;
and Garvey's apprehensions about "race suicide" have,
as we shall see, an altogether different context and meaning. In this context it is understandable why the type of
protest under discussion not only has been set in motion

by the legal inequality—which in fact unites all Negro opinion—but in addition has been focused so predominantly upon law and the acquisition of legal rights as the primary and even exclusive lever of social change. This becomes even more understandable when one realizes that for the past half century the context of Negro thought and aspiration has been one not merely of legal subordination but, rather, of something which is in fact more demoralizing. This has been a setback in public law. This setback may be identified as the series of three Supreme Court decisions, comprising the Slaughter-house Cases of 1873, the Civil Rights Cases of 1883, and the *Plessy* v. *Ferguson* Case of 1896, in which the Negro progressively lost ground that he had won after the Civil War. In the first decision, the Supreme Court held that the privileges-and-immunities clause of the Fourteenth Amendment referred only to federal citizenship (comprising such rights as free access to seaports) and not to state citizenship. In the second, the Court declared the Civil Rights Act of 1875, which had prohibited discrimination in places of public accommodation, unconstitutional. And in the third, the Court enunciated the doctrine of "separate but equal" which legitimated racial discrimination in law.[4]

The status of this doctrine as a reversal of a gain that had already been won; namely, the Fourteenth Amendment, and its effect as such upon race relations was, one may suggest, insufficiently appreciated before the school desegregation case of 1954 when the Supreme Court explicitly re-examined it in this light.[5] Before this one recalls that opinion inclined to the view that the *Plessy*

Case as well as the whole fabric of caste-like legislation that this hastened and solidified were simply an extension of sentiment originating in slavery and which had been temporarily suppressed by force of arms during the Reconstruction period.[6] To some degree this was encouraged by a radically depoliticized point of view within the social sciences at the turn of the century, of which Sumner is the example, a view that not merely taught that one cannot legislate against the mores but in addition perceived law and political action in general as emerging out of the sub-deliberative mores:

In our southern states, before the civil war, whites and blacks had formed habits of action and feeling toward each other. They lived in peace and concord, and each one grew up in the ways which were traditional and customary. The civil war *abolished legal rights* and left the two races to learn how to live together under other relations than before. The whites have never been converted from the old mores. . . . The two races have not yet made new mores. Vain attempts have been made to control the new order by legislation. The only result is the proof that legislation cannot make mores.[7]

Certainly from the vantage point not merely of contemporary thinking about constitutional law but of the new insights and new information of recent research on race relations, it becomes clear how deeply the "separate but equal" doctrine nullified that moderate formula for the Negro's acquisition of civil rights which had been voiced from the days of Lincoln's first expectations about the post-Civil War situation.[8] This formula, of which the Fourteenth Amendment was the keystone, was that racial negatives—that is, the racial category as such—would disappear from public law, which would then leave the way open for Negroes as they became qualified to avail themselves positively of rights enjoyed by others so qualified. Besides posing legal challenges, much of this would involve "testing out" of situations in the sphere of what is regarded as private social life. And if law cannot in a fundamental sense compel civility in this sphere, the effect for such civility of the illegal status of any public rules forbidding it is enormous. The prohibition of such public rules as illegal is a moral judgment about them. As such it deprives private action which conflicts not with the letter of the law but with its spirit of a public sanction. In putting a floor under what can be publicly done, it thus affects the moral atmosphere in which private or "social" action takes place. This atmosphere in turn influences the rate and direction of change. In permitting testing, it invites it. One successfully tested situation becomes a precedent established in opinion which then raises the floor upon which further testing can take place. It is by such a dynamic process that the absence of laws forbidding what is in the sphere of consent can impel change within this sphere and in a certain direction.

In these respects, C. Vann Woodward in his remarkable *The Strange Career of Jim Crow* has called attention to the social gains that Negroes continued to enjoy in the twenty years *after* Reconstruction had come to a close. This was a period during which Negroes rode in non-Jim Crow railway cars, ate in public restaurants—altogether a period in which some Southerners themselves took pride in the progress made in race relations. Woodward reports that as late as 1897, one year after *Plessy*, a Charleston editor wrote that a proposed Jim Crow law would be "a needless affront to our respectable and well-behaved colored people." [9] Woodward, to be sure, makes it perfectly clear that this was no golden age of race relations:

On the contrary, the evidence of race conflict and violence, brutality and exploitation in this very period is overwhelming. It was, after all, in the 'eighties and early 'nineties that lynching attained the most staggering proportions ever reached in the history of that crime. Moreover, the fanatical advocates of racism, whose doctrines of total segregation, disfranchisement, and ostracism eventually triumphed over all opposition and became universal practice in the South, were already at work and already beginning to establish dominance over some phases of Southern life. Before their triumph was complete, however, there transpired a period of history whose significance has been hitherto neglected. Exploitation there was in that period, as in other periods and in other regions, but it did not follow then that the exploited had to be ostracized. Subordination there was also, unmistakable subordination; but it was not yet an accepted corollary that the subordinates had to be totally segregated and needlessly humiliated by a thousand daily reminders of their subordination. [10]

We need not repeat here the details of his lucid account of those political and economic changes in the South which caused it to capitulate to racism and which caused the former allies of the Negro either to lose authority or to become transformed themselves into racists. It may suffice to point out that his findings preclude the understanding of the origins of legal segregation as simply derivative from a homogeneous array of Southern customs and mores. In enunciating the "separate but equal" doctrine, the federal judicature gave national sanction to and, hence, solidified the triumph of those forces in the South whose aims were clearly and openly stated to be not simply the separation of the Negro in an abstract sense but his subordination as well. The effect of the *Plessy* decision in nullifying the protection which the Fourteenth Amendment gave to the Negro was thus to spur the completion of a legalized caste system in which, as DuBois has said, the races become separated more completely and with greater humiliation to the Negro than was true in slavery itself.[11] Woodward notes that between 1900 and 1911 ten Southern states elaborated their laws requiring separation of races in transportation facilities, all of them including laws for street railways, and some for ferries and steamboats.[12] In legitimatizing racial categories in law, and hence the legislation of a caste line, the Jim Crow statutes destroyed the social validity of the Southern conservative's distinction which had begun to emerge in opinion between qualified and unqualified Negroes and his encouragement and support of the former. As such, the statutes deprived Negroes of any legitimate confidence that there was in fact a socially recognized relationship betwen effort and reward.

The aftermath then of the separate but equal doctrine is that the Negro in the South was faced on every side by a massive array of inequalities in law. As is familiar, the doctrine immediately collapsed in practice. The separate facilities provided for Negroes were not equal, even in the most visible external respects, which provided the basis for the first line of attack upon this doctrine. It later came to be argued that segregated facilities, regardless of parity in externals, were inherently unequal because of the psychological humiliation of being segregated.

What I believe this means is that it is politically humiliating for a race to be singled out as a category in public law when this race has no voice in the authorship of this law. And the fact that the enunciation of this doctrine went hand in hand with the virtual disfranchisement of the Negro needs to be hardly more than mentioned in passing.

This much may suffice to explain why the Negro's political goals have focused so squarely upon the courts as the means of restoring the color-blind Constitution, that is, the interpretation of the Fourteenth Amendment that is politically in harmony with the egalitarianism of the Declaration of Independence itself. In these respects the school desegregation case of 1954 restored and re-established this interpretation as the valid precedent. As we have seen, its implementation has been neither universal nor without friction. But the frustrations that this generates cannot gainsay the fact that this interpretation is a floor underneath and an impulsion toward change in the direction of its further implementation. Given the fact that perfect equality, not simply with regard to any particular class or minority group but in principle, is truly a utopian goal, the re-establishment of change in its direction is thus a politically decisive fact. To have the simplest estimate of its magnitude one merely has to realize the changes that would not have taken place in the South and the North had the Supreme Court sustained the separate but equal doctrine.

I suggest that it is only through realizing as clearly as one can why, in a specific context, the Negro protest should have focused upon segregation that one can see certain problems in this protest once the context changes or even begins to change. A main question—and one which is indeed arising out of the internal polemics of the Negro community itself—is whether integration, as a kind of cure-all, cannot become a narrow formula, and one which loses touch with the needs and mood of the Negro masses if not of Negro society altogether. So long as segregation was legal, the struggle for integration (or for desegregation) was primarily a struggle against the political humiliation of the Negro people as a whole— against the equivalent of the yellow badge. This type of struggle will continue, aimed not only at law but also at opinion, particularly with regard to public facilities and treatment, higher education, and job discrimination.

Let us leave aside any discussion of the serious problems of tact, priorities, where it makes sense for Negroes to concentrate their energies. A general but fundamental problem in this protest is that the logic, which made perfect sense when fighting against Jim Crow railway cars, can be turned against the very idea of a Negro community by interpreting any residential concentration among Negroes as "segregation." Now one may grant that such a community was historically rooted in and is sustained by discrimination. The fact remains, nonetheless, that for the foreseeable future not all but most Negroes will lead a separated social life if for no other reason than it is rooted in patterns of marriage. Yet, as stated earlier, the main stream of Negro protest—because of the existence of segregation statutes and practices the effect of which, in turn, has been to inflame a kind of doctrinaire commitment to an assimilationist thesis—found itself unable to argue simultaneously *against* Jim Crow and *for* the needs of a Negro community. But this means that it has trapped itself into a rhetoric where it is forced to conjoin its quest for the individual rights of Negroes to the premise that any co-existence among Negroes qua Negroes is degrading (because segregated) and hence a deprivation of equal rights. One can imagine the impression that this point of view as asserted by Negroes makes on whites. They may reasonably ask why Negroes should feel ashamed to live next door to other Negroes. The effect, of course, on the Negro masses who cannot escape the urban ghettos and who are implicitly being insulted by this point of view is that they can come to look upon such leaders not as seeking a juridically defensible right to live where they wish but rather as desiring to run away from the Negro community. Indeed, this point of view depreciates willy-nilly the efforts of Negroes to improve the quality of the life they lead with each other by "passing the buck" for all problems to segregation.

As we shall see, all this has been voiced by the Black Muslims who have reacted to the doctrinaire aspects of integrationism by an equally doctrinaire policy of anti-assimilationism or radical withdrawal, which at the same time seems to be oblivious to the importance of crucial civil rights and equalities. They nonetheless are of interest for opening a demand for what is a re-examination of a legalist formula. They also point toward the understanding that the quest for community and the quest for individual rights, far from being in conflict, can be seen to supplement each other when one transcends the plane on which these appear as polarities.

1. The ordination of Rabbi James William by Rabbi Wentworth Matthew.

2. Rabbi William being given his priestly charge by Rabbi Matthew.

3. Elder Harold Grey from Youngstown, Ohio, delivering a lecture.

4. Rabbi Small (*far left*) with the elders of the Congregation.

5. Rabbi Matthew praying over his wife.

6. (*Left to right*) Rabbis Matthew, Small, and William coming from the Harlem River after *tashlikh* ceremony on Rosh ha-Shanah.

7. Rabbi Matthew with graduates of the Hebrew school and elders (*in white*).

8. Rabbi Matthew addresses the graduates.

9. Rabbi McKethen, a representative of the Brooklyn group.

10. The Congregation attending Hebrew school graduation.

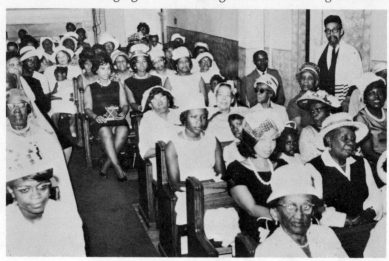

11. Rabbis Small and Matthew pose with cake commemorating Matthew's 74th birthday and the 50th anniversary of the Commandment Keepers.

12. (*Left to right*) A Commandment Keeper from Jamaica, Rabbi Small, Mrs. Matthew, Rabbi Matthew, all attending the 50th anniversary celebration.

SELF-HELP: THE QUEST FOR A NEGRO
COMMUNITY

Booker T. Washington. The career of Booker T.
Washington, including not only what he did and said
but also the way in which he came to be regarded by
Negro intellectuals, represents an interesting and important example of the way in which a definite impulse
toward self-help became distorted by the political facts of
his time. Washington was the only leader ever produced
by Negro society who enjoyed the respect of both the
politically mute Negro masses, then concentrated in the
rural South, and the leading whites, both in politics and
business, to whom he became *the* spokesman for Negro
affairs. He was the closest approximation which Negro
society produced to the Jewish *shtadlan* or Court-Jew of
the pre-emancipation period. As such he had an influence
and prestige in Negro affairs which no single individual
had ever possessed or, as Professor Frazier had pointed
out, will ever possess again as a result of the urbanization
of the rural Negro and his acquisition of civil rights.

Washington's life work centered around his foundation
of the Tuskegee Institute, in which, as the first such institution officered by Negroes, he saw his race on trial.
His work at Tuskegee was an application of the thesis
that the Negro could and should make himself wanted
by making himself useful:

In this address I said that the whole future of the Negro
rested largely upon the question as to whether or not he should
make himself, through his skill, intelligence, and character, of
such undeniable value to the community in which he lived
that the community could not dispense with his presence. I

said that any individual who learned to do something better than anybody else—learned to do a common thing in an uncommon manner—had solved his problem, regardless of the color of his skin, and that in proportion as the Negro learned to produce what other people wanted and must have, in the same proportion would he be respected.[13]

The clients of Washington's social work were the freedmen from the plantation and their children who, as he says touchingly in his autobiography, were so backward that they did not know how to care for their bodies, how to use a toothbrush; and, having been brought up on a diet of fat-pork, corn bread, and black-eyed peas, did not even know what constituted a healthy diet. His object was to train these people to develop vocational skills and the personal habits of a free man so that "they would be sure of knowing how to make a living after they had left us." His work was guided by a strong and explicit belief in the virtues of country and small-town life and the view that in large cities the lower classes were not only physically weakened and degraded by vices but also "tempted to live by their wits." More than this, his plans began with the recognition that 85 per cent of the Negroes in the Gulf states depended upon agriculture for their living. His goal was thus the preparation of teachers, in the broad sense of the word, who would transmit not only their skills but also their energy to these rural masses.. He avoided a curriculum which might cause his students to lose sympathy with country life and encourage them to emigrate to the cities. It is for this reason that he not only justified his very practical curriculum but also saw a danger in ambition which would estrange potential

Negro leaders from direct instruction of the rural masses. Beyond this, he did not think that Negroes would always be tied to the soil.

His standard of what he regarded as pleasant race relations was in fact an equal partnership: "In general, I found the relations [in Tuskegee] between the two races pleasant. For example, the largest, and I think at that time the only hardware store in the town was owned and operated jointly by a colored man and a white man. This copartnership continued until the death of the white partner." [14] Within this framework he was very much a "race man," who always spoke of "my race" with pride and, though it may seem but a small point, spelling the word Negro in his books with a capital "N" at a time when this was by no means universal usage. His rejection of colonization as a solution for the race problem, for example, begins with the following reflection:

Somebody also conceived the idea of colonising the colored people, of getting territory where nobody lived, putting the colored people there, and letting them be a nation all by themselves. There are two objections to that. First, you would have to build one wall to keep the colored people in, and another wall to keep the white people out. If you were to build ten walls around Africa today you could not keep the white people out, especially as long as there was a hope of finding gold there. [15]

If he were not averse to pointing out the shortcomings of his race in their present stage of progress from slavery in order to indicate its needs, he certainly did not fail to point out the contributions that the Negro had made in the past and would make in the future. He could look back upon the period of slavery, for all its injustice, as a school of civilization Having passed through this school, the American Negro was in his view fundamentally better off than his African kinsman who had never been fettered and never acquired civilization. But behind this comparison lay the expectation that the American Negro ultimately could go to Africa as a missionary or teacher to do social work and to bring to it the benefits of civilization. He was opposed to legal segregation as degrading to both races and thought that the disfranchisement of the Negro was unjust and would be a "sin that at some time we shall have to pay for." In *The Future of the American Negro,* first published in 1899, he asserted not only that the same tests and qualifications for the franchise should be applied to both blacks and whites alike but also that the black should give up none of his rights. Although he saw no wrong in the disfranchisement of ignorant and impoverished ex-slaves who, he thought, should not have been given the franchise in the first place, he did think they should then be provided with the education which would prepare them for the franchise:

Let the very best educational opportunities be provided for both races; and add to this an election law that shall be incapable of unjust discrimination, at the same time providing that, in proportion as the ignorant secure education, property, and character, they will be given the right of citizenship. Any other course will take from one-half your citizens interest in the State, and hope and ambition to become intelligent producers and taxpayers, and useful and virtuous citizens. Any other course will tie the white citizens of Louisiana to a body of death.[16]

The impression which has been permitted to grow about him that he was a compromiser who not only was prepared for the time being to give up equality but even accepted the white doctrine of the Negro's "place" is in complete contradiction with what he actually did and said. Perhaps the most familiar evidence for this is the statement in his Atlanta Exposition Address of 1895: "In all things that are purely social we can be as separate as the fingers, yet one as the hand in all things essential to mutual progress." [17] Given his published views on the impracticability of assimilation as a solution to the race problem in a milieu in which descent from a Negro classifies one as a Negro, this sentence, far from justifying legal and political inequality, was nothing more than a Southern Negro's way of telling Southern whites in broad daylight: we don't want to marry you. To regard his stress on duties and qualifications in itself as an indication of compromise is to invoke a conception of democracy or equality which abstracts, in a legalist spirit, from the question of the qualitative level at which this equality is to be maintained and sought.

The fundamental explanation, however, for the image currently held of him is the failure to appreciate the following fact. It was Washington's misfortune and, indeed, the misfortune of the whole nation, that the political fabric justifying his faith in this moderate program for the preparation of the Negro for both work and citizenship, collapsed within twenty years after its inception in 1881.[18] Washington, it will be recalled, stood for an educational and property qualification upon the right of suffrage that would be impartially applied to white and black alike. But this was precisely the standpoint of Wade Hampton and the Southern conservatives.[19] Such men

not only regarded the extension of the suffrage to the
qualified Negro as part of their duty and responsibility
to the Negro; in addition they saw in an alliance of the
educated and propertied of both races a basis for subordination of racial antagonism to the solidarity of a common class interest in areas that were heavily populated
by Negroes. As late as 1901, in the debates in the constitutional convention of Alabama which disfranchised the
Negro, the former governor Oates gave voice to that tradition. In Woodward's account:

> The indiscriminate enfranchisement of poor whites, believed
> Oates, was as vicious as the blanket disfranchisement of all
> Negroes, "the better element" of whom he would encourage
> to vote. *"It is not a racial question,"* declared the Governor,
> thereby denying the very premise of the whole movement.
> As for the low white man, "I would not trust him as quickly
> as I would a negro of intelligence and good character." [20]

So long as these men had been in control, Washington's
program for the Negro, far from being a compromise,
could realistically hold out to the Negro the promise of
an increasing measure of civic equality. What he did not
count on, certainly at the beginning of his career, was the
political collapse which induced Southern conservatives
to desert the Negro as a means of subordinating class
conflict among whites. Once this took place he became
not so much a compromiser—for he never abandoned his
goals—as a petitioner (though, from his own point of view,
far in advance of Southern Negro apathy) in a situation
of declining public respect for the Negro. From his private correspondence: "I am almost disgusted with the
colored people of Georgia. I have been corresponding

with leading people in the state but cannot stir up a single colored man to take the lead in trying to head off this [disfranchising] movement. I cannot see that they are doing a thing through the press. . . . It is a question how far I can go and how far I ought to go in fighting these measures in other states when the colored people themselves sit down and will do nothing to help themselves. They will not even answer my letters." [21] But in the context of the post-*Plessy* collapse and as seen from the point of view of Northern Negro intellectuals, who in many ways were far removed from Washington's immediate problems, this tended to be forgotten and his program seemed only to urge Negroes to acquire qualifications at a time when qualified Negroes were being depressed into an inferior caste. The result of this is that his sober and necessary goals for the Negro became seen as opposed to the quest of the Negro's civil rights.

In addition, Washington's educational aims offended those Negroes who had made a mark in the world of arts and letters. To them his description of the Negro as in need of tutelage in the elementary practical arts was insulting and one likely to have a depressing effect upon the level of aspiration among Negroes.[22] In the polemics of the time it was asserted that his program ignored the needs of "the talented tenth" whom the intellectuals wanted to see leave the South and take up the cause of Negro rights. Washington's educational policy, to be sure, was an explicit reaction against the classical education which Northern idealists had brought to the freedmen immediately after the Civil War, which he regarded as useless for them. But his views on this matter, far from being grounded in any anti-intellectualism, or in a desire to train Negroes to be dutiful servants, or still less in any opposition to civil rights, were the result of a single-minded refusal to be deterred by any other consideration than that of the most urgent needs of the mass of rural, Southern Negroes. These needs, in his view, were for the formation of habits, the habits of a free man, which would enable the Negro to become independent and self-sufficient in both his inner life as well as his work. In his view this required a moral discipline and training, beginning with training in elementary habits of personal cleanliness, to bring into being energy and self-control.

Reasoning less from a theory than from his own observations, he concluded that the effect of a purely intellectual education upon people who had had no opportunity to acquire these habits in their home lives would be disastrous. They would not acquire these moral habits for which a purely intellectual education is no vehicle. And without them the motivation to acquire this education would be the spurious one of the prestige it could confer as an attribute of whites, a motivation that would easily be satisfied by the mere symbols of education. The total result would then be an absence of the moral habits which are the ground of self-respect on the one hand and a half-education or pseudo-education on the other. Washington's aim was to raise the standard of the Negro people as a whole, by creating a large class of yeomanry who would be part of the people and, hence, active models for them. They would be respected and have social authority in maintaining and diffusing the standards for which they stood. As such, Negro society would be a coherent society or sub-society that would contain its own sources of motion toward progress. As such, Negro society would be far healthier than if it were simply a mass of backward peasants with a small educated (or, perhaps, half-educated) elite, who for all their political indignation would be so alienated from the mass that they could not be models for them. Hence, they could only influence the mass at all by means of intimidation and ideology which are weak devices for producing inwardly accepted habits—a training.

Washington correctly foresaw that if American Negro society were in a condition of health, with the standards and self-restraints of civilization actively pervading the whole, the Negro would be able to face the white, outwardly and in his own estimation, as an equal or possibly a superior, and this by virtue not of mere law but of his intrinsically valuable accomplishments. If American Negro society is not in the pathological condition which afflicts almost all the underdeveloped countries today, with their tiny alienated elites, part of this good fortune is due to the foundations which Washington laid for his people. If his rhetoric seemed to hallow morality at the permanent expense of intellectuality, it must be recalled, first, that he saw the complicated relationship between the two with a subtlety that few of his contemporaries possessed and, second, that he was engaged in a polemic against powerful prejudices, both Negro and white, in both the North and the South. Just as there were those who were arguing only for a classical education, there were also those who were fearful of educating Negroes at all. If, in steering a course between these two prejudices, he seemed to exaggerate the virtues of modest practicality out of all proportion, among other things, to his own not inconsiderable learning, this was but rhetorical protection for a policy which coincided in any event completely with the needs of the rural Negro at that time. Behind this rhetoric there was never any doubt in his mind as to the height of excellence which Negroes, individually or collectively, could attain, for all he had to do was to look at himself.

NEGRO CULTURE AND HISTORY.   The efforts of Negroes to give substance to or even to transcend mere race consciousness by becoming aware of their possession of a culture and a history has had both popular and intellectual expressions. Of the former, the myths of the sects which are the subject of this study constitute what is perhaps an extreme case. As we have seen, and as we shall further discuss, they proclaim the recovery of a lost culture and a lost national identity and religion as a defiant response to their situation. Or, to put this in a more extreme way, they have tried to overcome the pain of not having a unique culture of their own—of which a religion and a political history are such characteristically essential elements—by constructing one. But intertwined with the myths of these particular sects are many elements, shared by other Negroes, which are not nearly so heterodox as the total pattern of the mythology. Among these, for example, is the veneration of Ethiopia, which up to the very present has long nourished the Negro masses. As Claude McKay put it: "To the emotional masses of the American Negro church the Ethiopia of today is the wonderful Ethiopia of the Bible. In a religious sense it is far more real to them than the West African lands from which most of their ancestors came." [23]

In addition, we note that until the colonial period in Africa was ended, Ethiopia was the only historic country on that continent which had withstood the partition of Africa among the colonial powers. A number of Negro religious and improvement organizations, other than the Black Jews, have had the word Ethiopia in their very name. The Ethiopian World Federation, for example, had vague cultural and political aims, and among other activities it conducted classes in the Amharic language.

Another element which is central to the Black Jews but which certainly has found popular expression outside it is the view that the black man in Africa was the creator of all civilization—including not only material culture but also moral, religious, and philosophical principles. We note, for example, the publication in 1910 of *The Black Man the Father of Civilization: Proved by Biblical History* by a writer named James Morris Webb. This theme in secularized form became central to the outlook of Marcus Garvey. As suggested earlier, this countervailing racism was a reaction to the upsurge of published and publicly uttered anti-Negro racism which took place in the first decade of this century. [24]

On an intellectual or academic level the book which is almost a program of this quest for a culture is W. E. B. DuBois' *Black Folk: Then and Now*, of which the title is a suggestive clue. In the preface DuBois states that judgment about the future social and political development of the Negro must depend upon a judgment about his past, and in these respects the prevailing view is that the Negro has no history. DuBois then accounts how he was awakened from the paralysis of this judgment:

Franz Boas came to Atlanta University where I was teaching history in 1906 and said to a graduating class: You need not be ashamed of your African past; and then he recounted the history of the black kingdoms south of the Sahara for a thousand years. I was too astonished to speak. All of this I had never heard and I came then to realize how the silence and neglect of science can let truth utterly disappear or even be unconsciously distorted.[25]

Chapter One, "Negroes and Negroids," opens with a scientific discussion of race in which DuBois asserts the standard anthropological maxim that there are no pure or homogeneous races and with regard to the main category of racial differentiation—skin color, hair type, nasal structure—that the races overlap and fade gradually into one another. This then becomes the point of departure of a curious polemic to prove in the first place that the ancient high civilizations in Africa were Negro or Negroid:

In this Eastern Desert dwell the Beja tribes who may represent descendants of those who in ancient times populated Ethiopia and Egypt. They are black and brown with curly or frizzly hair, and present many of the same types as American Negroes do today.

Of what race, then, were the Egyptians? They certainly were not white in any sense of the modern use of that word —neither in color nor physical measurement; in hair nor countenance; *in language nor social customs.* They seem to have stood in relationship nearest the Negro race in earliest times. . . .

Volney in the eighteenth century expressed the belief that the ancient Egyptians were Negroes, or at any rate, strongly Negroid. Recently, Ripley, in his *Races of Europe*, agrees with this fact.[26]

In Chapter Six, "The Culture of Africa," he turns from the high civilizations of antiquity to the so-called backward peoples. The task he sets himself is: "If we could have a scientific study of mankind in Africa . . . without the necessity of proving race superiority, without exaggerated consciousness of color. . . . " [27] The rest of the chapter is then a documentation of the wealth of African culture from the Cape to the Sahara in both material and nonmaterial aspects. A principal item is his discussion of iron: "Torday has argued, 'I feel convinced by certain arguments that seem to prove to my satisfaction that we are indebted to the Negro for the very keystone of our modern civilization and that we owe him the discovery of iron.' " [28]

The tortuous logic beneath this outlook, as contrasted with the validity of the discrete facts, may be sufficiently apparent to make clear why this program never really took hold among educated American Negroes. Curiously enough it is not very different in an over-all way from the point of view of DuBois' arch enemy, Marcus Garvey. But there is this difference. When Garvey, addressing the Negro masses, said that the Negro was the source of all civilization, he had in mind a physical model who looked like himself and his audience; and this sentiment was connected to a political impulse about the future of Africa. DuBois, by contrast, is much more theoretical and detached. But to begin by asserting that there are no pure races and to terminate with a racialist or racist catalogue of Negro "culture" is to lay bare the defensiveness and obsession with race that is behind this whole point of view. This is indeed the result of arguing against Gobineau and Madison Grant or even Ben Tillman on the

premises laid down by them. All in all, what this shows is
the vacuity of racialist "cultural history" as a source of
pride. To designate what are really the inventions of
mankind as the inventions of a particular "race" is essentially to invite the Negroes to identify themselves with
Neolithic man, in order to acquire political self-consciousness. Furthermore, the educated American Negro has had
a healthy instinctive aversion to the romanticization of the
"folk" and the pseudo equalization of cultures to which
this leads—and for a very sound reason. If the refutation
of the racism of the turn of the century depends upon the
view that all cultures are equal, then the culture which
asserts that there are unequal races has the same rank as
the culture which asserts the opposite. This is to say that
if racism cannot be refuted in full cognizance of the inequality of cultures, then it cannot be refuted at all.

When one turns from "culture" or "cultural history" to
the political history of the Negro in the United States
and to various kinds of ethnographic and sociological research guided by its questions, one is on much firmer
ground. For here the American Negro does have a history
and an experience that is his own in a clear-cut and meaningful respect. The researches of American Negro scholars
in this sphere have produced solid and important works.
The contrast between DuBois' own impressive study of the
Philadelphia Negro as well as Washington's *Story of the
Negro,* written in collaboration with Robert Park, and the
defensive tract noted above is instructive. With respect
to this sphere, DuBois' own maxim that the way in which
one looks at the past has bearing on the present and the
future makes eminent sense. As one may readily imagine,

however, this sphere also is hardly free of "touchy" issues. Among these, for example, was the issue as to whether there was a survival of the African cultural heritage with the extremes defended most prominently by Herskovits and Frazier. Herskovits' attempt to defend the view that the African heritage was not extinguished was interestingly an attempt to defend the dignity of the Negro. For, as he reasoned, the view that the Negro held on to nothing of his own rests on assumptions such as the Negro is so child-like that he easily adjusts, or he voluntarily abandoned his culture for the superior customs of his masters. Herskovits thus states that the myth of the Negro past (that is, the belief that the African heritage was lost) "validates the concept of Negro inferiority." [29]

To all this Frazier continually pointed out that the evidence of these survivals is to be found not in North America but in the West Indies and Brazil.[30] We need not go into further details here of this polemic. What is interesting in the context of the present discussion is Frazier's awareness that by facing the fact that the enslaved Negro was a broken man who had lost the inward support of his culture, one would have a more adequate understanding as to why there were no large-scale revolts, an understanding which fully preserves the dignity of the Negro but on a deeper and more thoughtful level.[31] Frazier makes it perfectly clear that there was a great deal of opposition to the slave regime but that it took the form of individual escapes.

There is now emerging a new and nondefensive mode of reflection about the American Negro's unique experi-

ence, of which Mr. James Baldwin's writing is an example.
We shall discuss this in the final chapter.

THE BLACK JEWS: WHAT'S IN A NAME?   The Black Jews
partake of this quest for inwardness and show the significance which satisfactions in this respect can have for
one's bearing and one's behavior. But they are of interest
because of an additional question they raise. Can the
Negro have any fundamental self-respect so long as he
conceives of himself as a race?

As is evident from their own words, the Black Jews are
almost wholly nonpolitical. The older men were inspired
by Garvey's Back-to-Africa Movement, and a few still
keep up a nominal affiliation with what is left of the
organization. For the most part the interests and activities
of the men, and certainly of the women, are absorbed in
their rituals and in their belief that they have recovered
their true name and language. The one practical activity
with which they are preoccupied is their housing development in Long Island. When I questioned the most vocal
female member of the group as to what she thought of
the NAACP, she answered:

Only God can break down race prejudice, and until God
sets up the Kingdom of Israel, there'll be no peace—until
Shiloh. The Gentile race is not going to have any peace. That's
my conviction as far as the Bible is concerned. When the
Meshiach [Messiah] comes, he will take care of the twelve
tribes of Israel and they are the ones who will have the government.

Her apocalyptic expectations go hand in hand with a
private retreat from the world as her additional comments
show:

My grandfather had always told me that Hebrew was his language. We had books at home about the Hebrew children and Hebrew people. When I came to this country from the West Indies, I didn't find anyone until someone invited me to come up to the synagogue. When I came there, I saw placards on the wall with Hebrew on them and I said to the rabbi, "Do you teach this?" and I began and here I am. I took private lessons from him and I believe I was the first black woman to teach Hebrew in the western hemisphere. Besides before I joined, whenever I lived in an apartment house, I hardly ever knew anybody in the house.

All my spare time is spent right here. I sew, crochet, study my Hebrew, because if you don't talk it, you always have to keep brushing up. And besides since I'm the teacher, I have to keep ahead of the students. I never go to movies. I don't mean they're bad for other people, but I just don't like them.

Even on the privatized level of this woman and others like her, it is impossible not to see the depth of the desire, when awakened, which the Negro can come to crave for pride. As we have seen, this is satisfied in this sect by a myth that gives to its believers an inwardness they never before possessed. In terms of this myth they have a new conception of themselves as no longer despised pariahs but rather as the chosen people, with a proud past and a triumphant future. Their blackness, from which they cannot run away, far from being something to be ashamed of in a white society, becomes the hallmark of a superior nation to which even those who robbed them of the self-consciousness of their true identity are bound to look up to. In rejecting what they define as the white man's religion, they express contempt for him by virtue of a contempt for what he holds most sacred and in so doing they assert a supreme independence of his moral and religious principles, hence of him. To be sure, this all rests on a myth; and what is mythical is not so much the assertion that the so-called Negroes are a chosen people of one designation or another but rather that they were prior to their enslavement in any sense a unified people. One need but recall the painful fact that the supply of slaves depended upon intertribal wars or slave-raiding expeditions to see what the myth actually cloaks. But if the "golden age" prior to enslavement is mythical, neither the "need" for the satisfactions bestowed by the myth (or some nonmythical equivalent) nor the perception of those facts about the condition of the Negro which brings this need into existence are mythical. In the concrete case there lies underneath the Black Jews' aversion to the name Negro not a myth but the realistic insight that the Negro in America as he is socially defined and as he conceives of himself has no inward or positive basis of self-enclosure. His tribal or political identities, loyalties, languages, traditions, and cultures were all effaced, which leaves the consciousness of "race" as the unifying factor. To begin for the moment at merely the surface of conventional opinion, the Negro is defined as something negative, to be precise, a "non-white," in a way in which a white is not a "non-black." To be non-white, as is familiar, seems to have the "taint" of socially known descent from non-white blood.

Racial categories today are such a normal feature of scientific work in physical anthropology that one can easily become insensitive to the abnormality involved in *socially* defining and treating any group as a race, let alone one which is as racially heterogeneous as is the American Negro. Given the fact that people naturally define themselves by their countries or their gods, the emergence of a definition in terms solely of bodily criteria is something that has to be explained. The sects in proffering such an explanation are thus grounded in a scientifically correct insight about the condition of the Negro. When Matthew states that "Negro is the name of a thing," he has in fact surmised what is the key to this whole process.

In his lucid account of American slavery, Stanley Elkins has shown that slavery in its beginnings in the United States was neither racial nor chattel bondage. While most of the agricultural laborers coming into the colonies were in fact white indentured servants, there were Negroes among them who were, at least in law, assimilated to this status.[32] Beginning around 1660, however, a change occurred in the character of American slavery which caused it to be differentiated not merely from Latin American slavery but, perhaps, from any other form of slavery that ever existed. The primary cause of this is that rights in property as contrasted with social duties and restraints acquired a hegemony in the English-speaking world which they never possessed in Latin America where the church and the monarchy had an authoritative voice on behalf of traditional duty and against the pre-eminence of a capitalist class. The spirit of capitalism, by which I mean the emancipation of acquisitiveness and rights in property from moral and ethical restraints, triumphed in the Anglo-Saxon world with a comprehensiveness which was impossible in Latin America, for in the former the church was under the control of the planter class and the monarchy was interested in tobacco revenues.[33]

In describing the pre-Civil War situation in the United States, people very commonly oppose the capitalistic North to the anticapitalistic, traditional, patriarchial, even "feudal" South. This is perfectly legitimate, as Kenneth Stampp makes clear, for those few plantations whose owners had for personal reasons abandoned commercial goals.[34] But to make these few exceptions the standard for the whole is to overlook the fact that slavery in the South in its predominant mode—a predominance that is seen not merely in numbers but in the weight of the most influential voice behind Southern policy—was a profitable business, profitable enough to attract Yankee capital and energies. The plantation was a capitalistic enterprise in which the interests of the slave had to find an uneasy support as a species of valuable property but in a setting in which the maximation of the planter's money profits was a respectable aim.[35] This is not meant to suggest that a society which is pervaded by the spirit of capitalism must necessarily culminate in slavery or even wage slavery so long as the moral and political restraints upon these can and will arise. And it is indeed the essence of modern capitalism that it has arisen in a political democracy with a natural rights basis which has been a principal source of the check upon the very freedom it created. It does mean, however, that where slavery gets any kind of foothold at all in such an atmosphere, at least some if not most owners of slaves will have the strongest possible propensity to assimilate their ownership in slaves to property in general and to demand on the grounds of legal consistency the same measure of rights over their slaves that they possess with regard to their nonhuman property. Should they acquire these rights, this then can force or at least permit other owners of slaves who may have qualms about treating humans as property, but who are competing with the former in the same system, to follow suit. Even where private sentiment regards the full implications of such a legal fabric as morally repugnant and will not act to take advantage of its permissions, the contents of what is publicly legal, particularly when it is backed by powerful interests, affects the moral authority of these sentiments and the degree to which they can speak out against the law. Such a development took place in the United States.

As contrasted with Brazil, where the slave had a right to marry, to do some work for himself, to buy his freedom, the slave in America became divested of all those rights.[36] As the legislatures and courts systematically "rationalized" the full implications of what it was to be a chattel—of which process the *Dred Scott* Case may be seen as the ultimate deduction—the slave became as totally subject to the master's power as the law, which prohibited murder and severe cruelty but withheld from the slave the right to testify against his master, could allow.[37] But this occurred only with Negroes.[38] The racial factor, on which an ideology of inherent inferiority could be built, was a perfect correlate of the transformation of the slave from a person with some rights that he could autonomously assert to a chattel. Racial descent and chattel status thus coalesced in law which in turn stabilized public opinion.[39] As Chief Justice Taney wrote in his opinion in the *Dred Scott* Case, the Negro "had no rights which the white man was bound to respect." [40]

The decisive characteristic of the status of chattel was the legal and conventional deprivation of any right to a change in the status, culminating in emancipation. Baptism was at an early date adjudged to confer no such claim which eliminated the opposition that existed among the planters to the conversion of the slaves. (Southern church leaders in fact came to argue that the gospel would bring about "good conduct among Negroes." [41]) Neither did white blood which would have undermined the conception of the female as property which gave the owner property rights in her issue.[42] In this lies the origin not only of why the "taint" operates in a one-way direction but also of why sexual union between a free (white) female and a Negro (slave) male became so tabooed. As one may expect, the free Negro, and particularly the free mulatto Negro who was neither property nor black, was the indigestible element in the system. As the system became more and more defensive shortly before the Civil War, it is not surprising to find that the number of manumissions radically declined, were inhibited by law, were attended with the requirement that the freedman depart the state for a free state, and proposals to re-enslave the free Negroes were openly advocated.[43]

Thus, built into the conventional meaning of the term Negro, which was not even normally capitalized until 1929, was the association between "race" and the status as mere property and a set of presumptions about Negroes which make them seem fit for this status as mere property. The most important was that they are children who do not even know or care to know who their ancestors are, and accordingly have no self-restraints. Hence they are not qualified to possess the rights of adult man. Thus correlated with the objective powerlessness inherent in their status as mere commercial property was the subjective weakness of not having the inner support to one's pride and dignity that comes from social memories to oppose to this degradation. All this, again, stands in stark contrast to the situation in Brazil where not only was the slave, though owned, nonetheless a person with legal and conventional rights but where, in addition, the tribal cultures were not wiped out. It is also worthwhile to point out that the term Negro has had a different career in Brazil and never became normalized or respectable, being applicable only to unassimilated and lower-class blacks. In the reduction of the Negro in North America to a "race" or, as it is sometimes technically described, a social race lay his loss of inner independence as a people which made possible his acquiescence in a loss of external independence. It is along these lines that one can understand why resistance of the slaves to the slave regime, which was certainly great enough to produce demands for vigorous enforcement of a fugitive slave law, did not, however, issue in effective slave revolts such as occurred in Brazil.

To the extent that the Negro accepted the conception of himself which evolved under the slave regime, he acquiesced in that horizon within which his "racial" inferiority was a starting point. His reactions to the burden of looking at the world through this horizon have been varied. A primary one, originating in slavery, was to be overwhelmed by it and simply to act in accordance with a loss of both external and inward independence.[44] The Sambo, which as Elkins has pointed out emerged only in the United States, was an adaptation to a situation of a person who without rights, property, and power could by playing the part of a child manipulate the power holders to gain things for himself. He could "get away" with tricks, so long as he played this part, knowing that even if he were caught, he would get only the punishment of a child.[45] And, in general, one can link to the Negro's lack of any genuine independence all those modes of behavior which taken together constitute the stereotype of the demoralized Negro: sexual promiscuity, laziness, emotionalism in religion, childlikeness. As Washington said, slavery was not calculated to inspire the slaves with a love and respect for labor. When this behavior became not merely expected but rationalized into a double moral and legal standard, the way was open to abandon the Negro community to lawlessness.[46] The assumption by white police that Negroes were all children and the indifference that this would bring about to purely intra-Negro crime undermined the moral authority of those Negroes who stood for self-restraint. Hence, this weakened the ability of such Negroes to control the demoralization within their own communities. They would be ridiculed for trying to act like whites; and behind this ridicule is the knowledge of what the whites actually thought of them and were prepared to do for them.

A second reaction to the opinion of Negroes as racially inferior has been resentment—hatred of whites for treating and regarding them as inferior or at least an intensive self-consciousness or sensitivity about their racial identity, not unlike that of other minorities. But in the absence of an inner support such as would be derived, for example, from membership in a nation which could wage effective war against its enemies, there is a tendency for this resentment to collapse into self-hatred. A genuinely self-sufficient person would be psychologically indifferent to the praise or disrespect of others except as facts to be dealt with in a prudential manner. Without the basis of this self-sufficiency, hatred against being treated as a Negro can result in hatred of being a Negro. The most immediately relevant index of this is the absence of respect for and trust in Negro authority—the feeling that if an institution is run by whites it is better.

The third reaction to the structure of opinion about him constitutes all those attempts on the part of Negroes to transcend the horizon altogether that the self-consciousness with racial difference brings about. This includes not only the longing for national freedom that came to a head in the Garvey movement and the nationalist religious sects but also all those efforts to supplement race-consciousness by a consciousness of a common culture as defective as all these efforts up to now may have been.

In the light of these broad distinctions one can see that the essence of the kind of nationalism for which the Black Jews stand flows from their recognition of this fact. Connected with but also over and above the merely legal position of the Negro in America is the fact that he faces an opinion about himself that is humiliating. The core of this opinion, from their own point of view, is seen in their aversion to the very name Negro. As they themselves say, so long as the so-called Negro accepts the definition of himself as a mere race, he can never feel an inward equality with whites. This is so because he is admitting, through this conception of himself, that he has no culture of his own and is dependent for this upon whites. Their goal is thus not merely legal equality between white and Negro, preoccupation with which plays very little role in this sect. It is, rather, that subjective fortification which they think can only come from having one's own culture, conceived of as a national identity, religion, and language. It may be of some interest to emphasize this last point, although we shall return to it later. This is so because there are many students of the Negro problem who would agree with the implicit premise of the Black Jews that these are the three necessary elements of a culture. But precisely on the basis of these criteria they would argue that the Negro does not have any rational basis of a common culture.

But to return to the Black Jews we may say that, given the emphasis which morality has in this sect, their overall aim is nothing less than an attempt to purge the Negro of the remnants of the Sambo in the soul. Their explicit opposition to ecstatic religion—"niggeritions"—as well as juvenile delinquency and the improverishment of paternal authority shows very clearly what they are trying to dissociate themselves from. They are thus seeking to remoralize the lower-class Negro and in a way which disconnects this quest for excellence from any overtones of disloyalty or self-hatred. The vehicle of this is the myth which enables them to look at the demoralization of the Negro lower class as a deviation not from white society but, rather, from their own primordial moral integrity, a deviation which as they contend was caused by white society which enslaved black men and turned them into children. With a feeling of national pride engaged in the support of morality, they have the strongest inducement to repudiate the habits and the whole way of life of the demoralized segment of the Negro lower class. In all this they are really following the spirit and the counsels of Booker T. Washington. But there is this difference in orientation, if not about a matter of fact. For by explicitly despising these habits as things for which white society is to blame, they can look at themselves as adult human beings who do not owe their humanity, and this means their fundamental principles of right and wrong, to whites. Having recovered "their own," they can feel that they have emancipated themselves.

MARCUS GARVEY: POLITICAL NATIONALISM.[47]   Booker T. Washington addressed himself to the interests of the rural, Southern Negro whom he wished to become self-sufficient and to remain in the South. Marcus Garvey's following consisted of the urbanized masses who had been drawn to the metropolises of the North during World War I and found in these cities a freedom for the propagation of anti-white nationalism that they had never possessed in the South. If Washington enjoyed the sober respect of the rural Negro who got a vicarious gratification out of the fact that he had been invited to the White House, Garvey electrified the Negro masses by making them proud to be Negroes, not merely for emulating the achievements of whites but also, as he taught, because they were superior to whites. The blacker they were, the better. Garvey's program failed. But the ideas to which he gave such forceful expression, particularly the conception of the Negro as a dignified being whose dignity was fundamentally in-

dependent of white civilization, not only survived but, as
we shall see, still have a vitality in the Negro world today.

Garvey's main assumption, from which he derived his
program, was that race relations in the United States were
a state of war. Indeed, to judge from the wave of lynch-
ings and race riots which followed World War I, this was
not altogether hard to believe. And for Garvey all whites
were fundamentally alike. The white who abstained from
joining the Klan did so because he was too cultured; but
covertly they all had the same contempt for the Negroes
as an inferior race. Garvey's reaction to the racism which
he imputed to all whites was his construction in doctrine
of a countervailing racism. Black is good and white is bad,
of which the primary inference was an extraordinary
stress on the importance of racial purity coupled with an
attack on "miscegenation and race suicide." That he at
once set himself in opposition to light-skinned Negroes
is quite evident. It is also not surprising to find that he
saw some value for the Negro in the existence of the
Ku Klux Klan, on the expediential grounds that it would
drive the Negroes into an awareness that this was really
a white man's country and hence drive Negroes into that
kind of organized activity which would enable them to
rescue themselves from their despised condition. He in fact
went to Atlanta to confer with a leader of the Klan to see
if he would support his Back-to-Africa program.[48]

Coupled with this countervailing racism was an invocation of history to prove that the Negro and Africa
were the source of all civilization and culture. This too in
its own way was a counter-ideology against views then
current about the racial inferiority of the Negro.

We are proud of our racial lineage because out of Africa has come the civilization of the twentieth century. It is true that the twentieth century is corrupt and about to destroy itself, nevertheless the good that is to be found in it can be traced to the time when our ancestors held up the torch of science when the rest of the world was still in barbarism.[49]

Also, in his glorification of blackness, Garvey declared that Christ was a black man and sought to change those symbolic representations which took whiteness for granted as the ideal. The depiction of angels as black and even the manufacture of black dolls were prompted by his movement.

These sentiments, as may be apparent, are the common property of all the nationalistic sects. It will be readily understandable why the Ethiopian Hebrews, in spite of their failure to persuade the Garveyites to drop the name Negro and to adopt Judaism as their true, ancestral religion, were very much at home in this movement. In fact, the race leader whom Matthew most admires, next to Booker T. Washington, is Garvey. But for Garvey these sentiments were only a propaedeutic for a grandiose political goal: "The Redemption of Africa"; and it was indeed the projection of this goal that enabled him to organize what became a mass movement.

Garvey's political ideas—essentially an adaptation of the key ideas of the Jewish thinkers Pinsker and Herzl—were, when one eliminates the melodramatic flourishes, that the United States was a white man's country for all its professions of universalistic right.[50] As such the Negro could never be more than a second-class citizen until he lived in a country in which he controlled the government, that is, a country which was unambiguously "his." Until that time he would never gain the respect of the nations. To this end he organized his Universal Negro Improvement Association, to promote emigration back to Africa, and a shipping line, to carry passengers and freight both to Africa and throughout the world of Negro settlement.

As is familiar, the movement and the man himself after a moment of glory came to a sordid end. First, the Republic of Liberia, which had agreed to his plans for a colonization scheme and a rehabilitation loan, was unwilling on second thought to be host to a movement which included among its aims the emancipation of native tribes and which thus might cause those features of its social structure depending upon the use of compulsory labor to collapse.[51] It is also possible that there were pressures on Liberia from the colonial powers which were unwilling to see a beachhead of Negro nationalism established anywhere in Africa. Second, the financing of his project was completely erratic. Isolated from respectable business and without any real experience, he was sold overpriced and unseaworthy ships; and his ambition and his haste led him into dubious practices in corporate finance. He was in fact finally indicted by the federal government for using the mails to sell fraudulent stock, convicted and, after two years in jail, deported.

For many years it was common to see him written off as a glorious crank but one who showed the maladjustment of the urbanized masses.[52] Today I believe he is no longer viewed quite in this way. Without minimizing the genuinely erratic aspects of his program, it is possible—as does Edmund Cronon in his excellent study, *Black Moses*—to see not merely a certain sense that he was making but also some solid achievements and precedents from which the American Negro can and has benefited. In the first place, it is a misunderstanding to think that he seriously contemplated the emigration of every American Negro back to Africa. Beneath his flamboyant rhetoric, which included the foundation of the Empire of Africa in 1921 and the inauguration of himself as provisional President, lay a plan for a modest colonization scheme. It was this that was frustrated by the political situation of his time, a frustration which his rhetoric may have in part abetted. Had he lived twenty-five years later, and hence that much closer to the end of colonialism, he might well have become a nationalist leader in his own Jamaica where there would have been a greater congruence between his powers and his ends. To take the Negro population not merely of the United States but of the whole world as his electorate led him into becoming a sensational propagandist which neutralized not so much planning as sober planning. The life of the movement became dependent upon immediate results and also upon the fate of one charismatic leader. Even so, he may have constituted an influence toward national liberation in the former colonial powers that was greater than he realized.

What was his influence upon American Negro society itself? Among the most interesting and important features of his movement were the lessons that could be drawn from his business enterprises, which included the shipping line, cooperative housing, restaurants, laundries, and so on. The impulse behind these, of course, was the pure spirit of Booker T. Washington—a man publicly admired by Garvey—but transferred to the urban North and thus completely disconnected from the imputation of political surrender which Negro intellectuals had foisted upon Washington's advocacy of Negro enterprise after the Negro had been disfranchised. For Garvey the demonstration by Negroes, both to whites and to themselves, that they could run a real business was an obvious source of race pride. What Garvey did in fact was to explode or, perhaps, to correct what has been called by Frazier the myth of Negro business which is, as he described it in his *Black Bourgeoisie,* the view that the Negro could achieve economic salvation through individual entrepreneurship.[53] Garvey's experience certainly bears witness to those very obstacles to entrepreneurship that Frazier thought decisive—lack of capital, business tradition, those social connections which bear on the success of business enterprise, and the distrust if not ridicule of other Negroes. But on the other hand, it also points to the fact that an ideology together with an organization can do things which individual entrepreneurship among Negroes cannot achieve. Both Garvey's failures and successes in business enterprise point respectively to the perils as well as to the possibilities inherent in this combination.[54] We have noted the housing development of the Black Jews, where the group collectively bought a tract of suburban real estate, which partakes of this impulse. As we shall see it is present among the Black Muslims on a much larger scale.

AMERICAN COMMUNISM AND THE FORTY-NINTH STATE. The Communist line in behalf of a self-governing Negro republic in the black belt is a relic of prewar discussion about territorial autonomy that deserves brief mention. The line was short-lived. It was launched at the Sixth

World Congress of the Communist International, held in Moscow in 1928, as "the right of self-determination of the Negroes in the Black Belt," and was called off in 1935, to the great relief of Negro Communists, after the United States had recognized the Soviet Union. In subsequent pronouncements about Negro rights, particularly after Russia was invaded, the *Daily Worker* declared that to fight segregation in the armed forces at this time was appeasement.[55]

On the whole the only people who really cared for this line were Communist intellectuals and mainly white ones at that who saw in the idea of a self-governing republic another Birobidzhan. In the Negro world it was received much the same way in which all such schemes emanating from whites, including proposals for emigration, have always been received. "We maintain that the mere existence of the proposal proves that the idea of separation is uppermost in the minds of the red brain trust and not the idea of oneness, and in advancing this theory of separation the Communists are hand-in-hand with the southern ruling class." [56]

The National Movement for the Establishment of the Forty-ninth State was a prewar splinter of Garvey's U.N.I.A. which sought to establish not a republic but a state in the unpopulated Southwest. As Myrdal indicated, it never amounted to anything.[57]

THE BLACK MUSLIMS.   The Black Muslims* constitute a culmination and a new development in the progression

---

* This is not strictly the sect's own name for itself, and I use this term only because it has become so much a part of general property. These people call themselves "Temple of Islam" or "Muslims" (pronounced "Mooslims").

of phases thus far outlined. This includes the protest against inequality, the self-discipline and enterprise of Washington, the rejection by the Black Jews of Christianity and their assumption of a preslave nationality and religion, the political orientation of Garvey, and the turning from Africa to the United States in raising the demand for territorial autonomy.[58] As to this last point, the Muslims are admittedly vague and refuse to be drawn into premature specification. The crucial innovation of the Muslims is the political propagation of what amounts to a sociological theory about why the Negro has no self-respect, reminding one of the propositions if not the tone of the Jewish Zionists. This doctrine is not original, it is found explicitly in Garvey's opinions and implicitly in all the nationalistic sects. In fact, the experience of the minority is so sharp that one may well doubt whether there is any position that has not been conceived of and thought over before. Nonetheless, what is novel is the rhetorical emphasis given in this sect to the doctrine that the Negro feels inferior because he is inwardly enslaved to the idea of white superiority, a rhetoric directed toward creating in the Negro a kind of mass self-awareness about this condition.

As already mentioned, the Black Muslims in their earliest phase, when they still called themselves "Moors," were as apolitical as the Black Jews and Coptics. In fact, the Moors exhibited even a hyperintensification of one of the apolitical features of these sects, that is, of the magic-cult.[59] There was as among the Black Jews a procession of prophets, beginning with Noble Drew Ali, preaching the same type of doctrine about the need for the so-called

Negro to recover his true name in order to recover his powers, the same preoccupation with disease and poisonous foods. The main beliefs of the Moors, for example, as summarized in Fauset's description, were as follows:

Before you can have a God, you must have a nationality. Noble Drew Ali gave his people a nation (Morocco).
There is no Negro, black, colored, or Ethiopian—only "Asiatic" or Moorish-American.
The name means everything; by taking the Asiatic's name from him, and calling him Negro, black, colored, or Ethiopian, the European stripped the Moor of his power, his authority, his God, and every other worthwhile possession.[60]

The Moors, to be sure, immediately got into difficulties with the police in Detroit, but this seemed to be due less to their anti-white militancy than to the fact that they were suspected of practicing human sacrifice. But one has only to compare the account of the Moors as given by Erdmann Beynon, significantly called "The Voodoo Cult among Negro Migrants in Detroit," with the accounts of the Black Muslims of Lincoln and Essien-Udom to see what a vast change has occurred. In Beynon's paper there is hardly a shred of evidence to suggest that they could ever be a political force, anything other than an erratic but interesting sect for uprooted people.[61]

Now the more developed "Muslims" preserve all the features of the earlier myths, including the following doctrine:

The so-called Negro is a blood-descendant of the original man. Who is better knowing of whom we are than God himself? He has declared that we are descendants of the Asian Black Nation and of the tribe of Shabazz which came with the earth when a great explosion divided the earth and the moon sixty-six trillion years ago.[62]

Nonetheless, in analyzing the pronouncements of the intellectuals who have become spokesmen for this movement, particularly those who travel around the country talking on college campuses, one gets the striking impression that these intellectuals believe no more in this science fiction than do their audiences, because among other things they hardly refer to it in serious discussions with educated people. They have the same aversion to the name Negro with which we have been familiar thus far, and on the grounds that it is a humiliating, non-national, racial designation, evolved in slavery and imposed on them by whites. Nonetheless, one has a strong impression that what they really want to be called is not so much "Muslim" as black men, and that they are gradually preparing the way to drop the irrationalities in the sect altogether including, perhaps, the identification as Muslim.[63] Thus a kind of "stratification" in doctrine has emerged, the original name-magic for the primarily old and uneducated, onto which has been′ superimposed a thoroughly secularized doctrine about the condition of the Negro, its causes and its cure, for those who are younger and more educated. It is certainly on the basis of the latter that they have been able to augment their membership.

This doctrine, when clearly isolated from the mythological elements that are primarily for internal consumption, is a reworking of Garvey's basic thesis that racial relations are a state of war but focused upon a domestic American context. Its main tenets are that the Negro in

America is looked down upon as an inferior race—as proved by the fact that whites do not want to intermarry with them. But the Negro, because of all those features of his history which caused him to be regarded and to regard himself as a "race," that is, a "non-white," feels inferior. Thus he is inwardly enslaved to a belief in white superiority, that white is good and black is bad, of which the most superficial manifestation is the preference in the Negro world for the white physical model itself—the disdain for kinky hair, the very term "good" hair, the esteem for light skin color, the "blue-vein" societies, and so on. As such he secretly desires to be white, which leads him to value acceptance by whites as something good in itself. More than this, to the extent that he tries to delude himself with the view that he is no different from any other American, he comes even to demand this acceptance as a right. But the more he demands it, the less he will be respected; for over and above the fact that whites will still look at him as a Negro is the fact that people will not respect those who have no self-respect.

The Muslim solution to this diagnosis of the Negro's psychological problem is that the Negro, in the face of this opinion, should turn his back on white society, form his own community from which *he* excludes whites, and as such recover his independence and self-respect. Whites are not allowed to visit meetings of the Muslims and intermarriage is ground for immediate exclusion from the sect. What is more, the Muslims have spoken out against the mass sit-ins in restaurants and stores, contending that the Negro in so doing is merely forcing himself into a place where he can spend money to make a white man richer.[64] The question of whether they think it is right that Negroes be excluded from public institutions is not raised in a dialectical manner in the kind of discussions they conduct. Apart from the mythology, which is similar enough to that of the Black Jews and Coptics to make it unnecessary to go into details, the life within the sect is sustained in the first instance by speeches about the injustice of the white, the weakness of the white, and eventual black supremacy in both the United States and the world. The Muslims, as indicated above, have prudently refrained from committing themselves to any program requiring immediate results. Another important element, in fact the quintessentially secularized element in their altogether secularized doctrine, is their explicit attack on the pariah notion that in the next world the last will be first and the first will be last. To this the Muslims say that the world is "this world." This attack distinguishes them very much not only from ecstatic religion of the Holiness type but also from the other nationalistic religious sects such as Black Jews who, while sharing with the Muslims the aversion to extreme emotionalism in worship, have by no means gone this far.

All in all, then, the Muslims stand for the view that the Negro is at least as good as the white, not because he is a man too and as such equally entitled to the same rights enjoyed by whites but, rather, because he is black and black is good. The logic of their doctrine has the intention of catapulting the Negro upward onto a plane where he no longer feels it necessary to disprove to himself the old ideology used to justify slavery, that is, that the slaves were not fully human. His new-found self-esteem at least seeks to put him above the very need to acknowledge this opinion. As stated above, this is achieved in this sect by hammering away at the theme that the Negro throughout his whole history in the United States has been plagued by a feeling of inferiority, and by a militant anti-whitism centering around the theme that whites are enemies and cannot be trusted and hence aimed at dissolving the confidence which the Negro has in the white man. Self-hate in this sect seems to be corrected primarily by hatred of others. This distinguishes the sect not only from Zionism but also from Garveyism which with all its anti-whitism—much of the same as is to be found in this sect—nonetheless had in its majestic political goal a basis of self-sufficient pride that transcended mere hatred of whites. Thus the militancy of the Black Muslim seems to be founded on a very self-conscious orientation to the opinion of whites after all.

It would be a serious mistake to minimize the potency of their outlook, even with these qualifications, in creating a feeling of independence from white society. The Black Muslims claim that the Negro is "brainwashed," "mentally dead," and their anti-whitism may indeed have the effect that they seek in its use as a kind of "counter brainwashing." But it would be a much more serious mistake to disconnect the anti-whitism, which is entirely verbal, from their attempts to lay the basis of self-sufficiency, not merely by means of a mythology but by the construction of a moral community, in activities and institutions, in which a Negro can trust another Negro. And, indeed, as Essien-Udom reports it, the Muslims believe that "accepting the idea of total separation of the races aids the Negro in ridding himself of the belief that the whites are solely responsible, and are to be continually held responsible for the Negro's 'degradation and miseries.'" [65] In short, to their proposal that the Negro turn his back on white society, they offer him, so to speak, somewhere worthwhile to go.

The "social" work of the Muslims is not unlike that of the Black Jews although it is much more extensive. Their educational institutions, for example, the various "Universities of Islam," are full-time projects. They do not want their children to attend the public schools because they do not want them to be exposed to the "white-man's history." The sect not only aims in general at the same type of remoralization as do the Black Jews but has in addition sought recruits among ex-criminals and even convicts. [66] As one can imagine, the rules are somewhat stricter and more comprehensive than in the other sects. Men are searched for weapons before they enter the "temples." Fornication is ground for dismissal from the sect for one year. The separation of the sexes in their temples and schools is severe and is more self-consciously connected with this problem than it is among the Black Jews where they are following Jewish custom. (The latter also do not require this separation except during the Sabbath services.) Even critics of the sect admit that they are able to control "vice." But as Essien-Udom has pointed out, the Muslim attitude toward sex, which is an interesting clue to their whole outlook, is by no means one simply of prudery. It is rather part of a forceful attempt to compel both Negro men and women of the lower classes to cease looking at one another through the eyes of whites.

A quotation from an interview he cites makes this perfectly clear: "Islam makes you appreciate black women. I appreciate my black women by showing them my politeness at its most highest degree [sic]. This applies mostly to Muslim women because a regular Negro woman would not understand such politeness. She would think that I was a queer if I tried to treat her nicely and respectfully." [67]

Now we turn to the real innovation of the sect. This is its decision to remain in the slums and to rehabilitate life in its very midst. The sect, which by virtue of its size has evidently a good deal of capital at its disposal, has bought and rehabilitated slum housing, lowered rentals, and plans to erect community centers. In a way the Muslims have in fact answered their claim for territorial autonomy. It is the Negro section of the city from which they cannot easily escape and which they intend to make livable.

NEGRO NATIONALISM AND
THE SOLUTION TO
THE NEGRO PROBLEM

IN THE PREVIOUS CHAPTER I sketched some key phases of Negro protest leadership. This culminated in a discussion of a militantly anti-white, nationalistic sect which enunciates a doctrine of radical withdrawal from white society as a solution to the Negro problem. In this final chapter I shall deal with the impact that this nationalism might have on Negro opinion and Negro leadership in the immediate future. As may readily be imagined, Negro society (white society, too) is baffled, embarrassed, even afraid of this nationalism. For a group of Negroes themselves to assert a policy of apartheid and to achieve, moreover, some success with it seems to threaten to overturn the apple cart. It is not surprising that many students of the Black Muslims, as of the Garvey movement before this, have attempted to "explain them away" as a fundamentally irrational phenomenon. As they see this movement, it is, indeed, an understandable response to racial discrimination but one which will disappear when discrimination disappears and the Negro is completely integrated into American society.[1]

One may easily grant the correctness of this conclusion and yet still maintain the following reservation: in an *a priori* manner it wholly excludes from serious consideration the possibility that there may be some validity and importance in the insights which the Muslims and the kindred sects might have about the causes of difficulties which the Negro has in being integrated into American society. Given the outward shell of the doctrines they proclaim, it is, of course, not hard to understand the disinclination to look beneath it. It hardly needs emphasis that few thoughtful people would regard as a solution to the Negro problem a doctrine that tries to solve an inferiority complex by hate, which if acted upon seriously would lead to a racial war that the Negroes would lose and which, in addition, rests upon a palpable mythology that no one—even in the sects—does not see through in some way. When I asked the leader of the Black Jews, for example, what he thought of the Black Muslims, he replied, 'They are just Negroes who don't want to admit that they're Negroes."

The question that thus arises is whether beneath or above the surface of the ideology there is some rational apprehension of the broad position of the Negro in America which makes sense and which, when separated from the racist and apocalyptic elements of the ideology, might impinge upon Negro opinion on this rational level. Now in seeking to understand the issues in the rational discussions which might emerge, we may recall the thesis that has been the point of departure for this analysis. Be-

cause of legal segregation, the idea of a voluntary Negro
community as a need and, hence, a legitimate concern of
American Negroes disappeared from respectable discussion. So long as Negro life was faced by compulsory, ex-
ternally imposed segregation, every movement toward
the formation of a self-respecting voluntary community
that would be the social matrix of the Negro's own impulses toward self-improvement was throttled. The objective legal situation brought into being an atmosphere
that suppressed the distinction between a compulsory
ghetto and a voluntary community, for there was, indeed,
no choice.

As stated earlier, Booker T. Washington was perhaps
the one important Negro leader whose program for the
Negro embraced the goals of both a voluntary community
and civic equality and who clearly saw the interdependence between these aims. We recall his statement in his
open letter to the State Constitutional Convention of
Louisiana that the permanent disfranchisement of the
Negro on a caste-like basis would "tie the white citizens
of Louisiana to a body of death." [2] His program, which
began almost twenty years before *Plessy* v. *Ferguson,*
demanded and depended, for its legitimacy within Negro
society, upon a political fabric in which the attainment
of qualifications would be followed by the attainment of
effective rights. When his program was carried on after
this political fabric collapsed, the autoemancipatory elements became discredited as "Uncle Tom-ism." In this
process of discreditation, the two goals of his program
split into two extremes and have remained, more or less,
in this condition to this very day. These extremes are a

doctrinaire individualism on the one hand, linked to an assimilationist theory in terms of which the existence of a Negro community can be described only as "a pathological form of an American community," and an equally doctrinàire nationalism or anti-assimilationism which repudiates hope for real civic equality and, hence, any rational political preoccupation with this goal.[3]

The classic example of the first is still the point of view put forth in Myrdal's *American Dilemma.* Myrdal, beginning his massive work in 1937, looked at the Negro problem, as did many other public-spirited students, within a horizon bounded completely by the post-*Plessy* collapse. Within this horizon the fact of legal segregation was the irreducible point of departure for the analysis of the entire Negro problem. From this point of view, the Negro problem, as Myrdal could say, was not a Negro's problem but a white man's problem, for the Negro's position is really determined by the opinions and actions of whites.[4] If whites think that Negroes are inferior, then Negroes will behave so as to conform to this expectation. If whites elevate their opinion of Negroes, or, as Myrdal puts it, "for some reason" mitigate their prejudice, then the behavior of Negroes will change to correspond with these new opinions, and whites will see Negroes in a new light which will be the basis of accepting Negroes as social equals if not of complete assimilation.[5] From this point of view the really reactionary element is the Negro who does not demand integration because he profits from segregation. As mentioned earlier, these might be incompetent Negro functionaries who have a guaranteed clientele so long as segregation exists. Without questioning the

fact that such private motivations can and do exist, it is
nonetheless interesting to point out that the only *primary*
role that the Myrdal thesis can assign to Negroes themselves in this process is the one of obstruction. In a positive
direction, that is, toward greater integration or assimilation, he can demand change, he can adapt to change; but
the change must be initiated by whites. The basic changes,
as conceived of in the Myrdal thesis, from which the
changes in the white evaluation of a Negro as a person
are expected to flow, are by and large formal or impersonal changes with regard to legal and political equality
and equality of opportunity in employment. Myrdal actually says that the original change can as easily be a
change of Negro standards as of white prejudice.[6] But
the examples he gives of these standards are family in-
comes, standards of nutrition, housing, health, and education which, as he himself asserts, derive from opportunities in employment. If there is any doubt as to which
in his view is the primary lever of social change, his
statement in another context makes this perfectly clear:
"It is thus the white majority group that *naturally* deter-
mines the Negro's 'place.' All our attempts to reach scientific explanations of why the Negroes are what they are
and why they live as they do have regularly led to *determinants on the white side of the race line*." [7]

One may grant the political truth of this point of view
at a time when primary facts were segregation statutes
made by white legislators which could be declared unconstitutional only by white judges. But looking at this thesis
almost a quarter of a century later, one can hardly avoid
seeing what it does to radicalize the Negro's temporal

dependence upon a specific set of white determinants into a universal. To the extent that this theory, which was given its form by the existence of segregation statutes, still has a hold in Negro opinion, it has the effect of corroding any civic spirit among Negroes on behalf of a Negro community. It almost, so to speak, enjoins dependence upon white society. The effect of this has been well described by Mr. James Wilson, who sees the power of this theory as one of the causes of the phenomena he notes:

Provident Hospital, an all-Negro institution in Chicago which is filled to overflowing with Negroes seeking medical aid, has great difficulty in raising its budget, and must rely heavily on white charity. The Joint Negro Appeal, organized to help support welfare services in the Negro community, experiences great difficulty in raising $25,000 from a community of 750,000 people. The local branch of the NAACP has until recently been unable to create and sustain even a modest staff of workers to deal with the problems which that organization attempts to act on. The Urban League, which for about forty years has provided a variety of services to Negroes which no other agency offered, could not in a typical year in the recent past raise $10,000 from Negroes as their contribution to a budget which was fixed at between $80,000 and $90,000. Although perhaps 300 Negro lawyers live in Chicago, the NAACP can rarely find more than three or four who will assist in the work of providing legal defense for Negroes who are the victims of racial persecution. Despite the fact that Negroes number about one-fifth of the total population of Chicago, and have in their midst one of the most powerful and well-organized political machines in the United States, the larger race problems rarely receive legislative treatment or even discussion from governmental authorities. No effective fair employment practices act exists; medical services are largely segregated; and the housing market is based on strong racial barriers.[8]

This radicalization of the idea of dependence, to the point where it legitimates civic apathy (at least for any other purpose than the self-liquidation of the Negro community) is one of the two principal elements in the doctrinaire individualism that emerged in the reaction to legal segregation. The other is its conception that the Negro problem will be solved by intermarriage and ultimate absorption of the Negro as an individual. This thesis is obviously nourished by powerful sentiments of opposition to racial bigotry. But beyond this it is also guided by what it regards as the objective view that there is no rational reason why the Negro in America should remain a Negro. Stripped of his African heritage, he has no culture, religion, language of his own that has not been acquired from whites. He has nothing pre-American in his culture. One could say that he is the quintessential American; and Myrdal could account for whatever differences there are in the ways of Negroes and whites by looking at the Negroes as "exaggerated Americans." (The possibility that whites in some respects may be exaggerated Negroes plays, as one may suspect, no part in this doctrine.) More than this, it would be alleged that the American Negro is racially so heterogeneous that the term American Negro is not even a clear-cut racial category. Moreover, given the fact that in the United States anyone is socially defined as a Negro who openly admits to Negro descent—and the proportions are unimportant—it will follow that there are many "so-called" Negroes who are biologically white.

A more important point, however, for the assimilationist thesis is the primary fact of the cultural *tabula rasa*. On this basis, it is posited that there can be no natural obstacles or resistances to assimilation with whites from within the Negro world because it is dependent upon the white world for its standards and values. Whatever obstacles there are lie primarily in the racist antipathies and prejudices of whites. There are, to be sure, class differences or educational differences within each race which would make for selective association across racial lines much as they would within them. Where there are no class or educational differences, there are no cultural differences that are due to race alone. Where social backgrounds are the same, any obstacles to association lie in fear, prejudice, a state of mind—primarily of whites, but also of Negroes who react defensively to the prejudices of whites by avoiding contact with whites. From this follows the social importance on the one hand of propaganda or indoctrination as a means of eradicating prejudice and on the other hand those actions which induce or even compel people to get close enough to one another so that they can see that there are in fact no cultural obstacles to association.

I think there can be very little scientific clarity in the study of race relations without recognizing the fact that assimilation, in the radical sense of biological absorption, is *the* solution to the Negro problem, as hypothetical as this may be. If Negroes could be absorbed, that is, if there were no Negroes, there would be no Negro problem. It is also important to point out that a state can regulate marriage, such as, for example, in setting a minimum age limit. In so doing it may find it necessary to conform to prevalent opinions as to who may marry whom, such as the opinions against polygamy and incest. Nonetheless, laws and opinions against interracial marriage are as much an abridgment of civic equality that is derived from the equality of natural rights of man as is the presence of any other racial category in public law.

But to see that biological assimilation is the theoretically elegant solution to the Negro problem is one thing. To think that this goal can be brought about by acting directly toward it is another thing which rests on an error of historical fact. It overlooks the fact that assimilation, as a social policy for absorbing culturally and ethnically differentiated minorities into the "host" society, was aimed at peoples who had a choice within their own powers whether to assimilate or not. The Jews are the classic case in point. From their own point of view their history in the diaspora has been a constant struggle to guard against the temptations placed in their way by the non-Jewish world to give up and become part of the nations. One has merely to remind oneself of the social privileges in periods of religious persecution that religious conversion would supply. But the situation continued throughout the post-Enlightenment period. In crucial respects enlightening despots such as Napoleon imposed citizenship upon the Jews who did not want it because it meant the destruction of their corporate communal life and their involvement in concerns which secularized them and thus weakened their attachment to the ancestral ways. Thus in both periods the privileges of full citizenship were a reward held out for those who were willing to assimilate and to pay, as it were, the price of giving up the basis of their minority existence. The situation of the Negroes in Brazil is not fundamentally dissimilar. There the African and pagan culture survived. And there too if the Negro were only willing to give up his language and religion and become Christianized, Europeanized, the way was open to high social mobility as well as to intermarriage (which ought to be seen, theoretically, as interdependent).[9] He could in fact cease being a "Negro," the term used in Brazil only for *unassimilated* blacks.

The American Negro manifestly has not had this choice. Paradoxically the absence of an African heritage, the fact that in a way the American Negro is less of an immigrant than any other group including the American Indians, has made it not easier but more difficult for him to be assimilated—as the contrast with Brazil makes immediately evident. For without this choice, which would give the Negro an objective basis of showing his reluctance to assimilate except on his own terms and where he chooses, the white, no matter how wildly and with what paranoid fears he may exaggerate this, sees the Negro as completely dependent upon him and wanting to fasten upon him like a starfish. At least from the white's point of view there is no psychological equality between the white and the Negro. And just as this imbalance can distort, kill, or mutilate love between two individuals, so can it do the same between the races taken together as wholes. Is it any surprise that the Black Jews and the Black Muslims have responded to all this with anti-white invective?

But leaving aside these psychological subtleties, let us simply remind ourselves of the social obstacles to intermarriage and of the fact that while intermarriage is increasing, it is still statistically insignificant and outside the big cities in the North practically unheard of. Why so? In the first instance, one might cite prejudice and I would include people's desire to have their children resemble them. Beyond this I would also note the point of view of whites who have no particular taboos, certainly no disinclination to having extramarital sex relations with Negroes but who are unwilling to bring into the world children who will be Negroes and who will therefore have less freedom than they themselves possess. To all this the proponents of the assimilationist thesis might argue that if more people were to intermarry, then the presence of interracial families would shock people out of their prejudices, cause them to become habituated to the normality of this arrangement, which in turn would bring about an augmentation of the number of intermarriages. However, it should also be mentioned that if the number were rapidly to rise in the immediate future, prejudices might be shocked in a way which would not dissolve them but strengthen them. But to raise some additional problems, I would note first of all that from brief observation of interracial families in Chicago, as contrasted with childless mixed marriages, they really feel at home in a society composed primarily of other interracial families and are not absorbed into either white *or* Negro society. Is this formation of a curious kind of ghetto really assimilation? It is not unlike the situation of those social circles in prewar central Europe composed mainly or exclusively of baptized Jews. More important, assimilation, even if it worked, would be a long-term process, beyond the foreseeable future. But what the Negroes want is a greater degree of equality and respect now. Are they to be asked to wait for such historical and sociological predictions about a far-off future to work themselves out? More important than even this is the fact that when the entire question is looked at from the standpoint of the present, that is, within the framework of an acting man, assimilation as an aim, suggested by certain legalistic approaches to race relations, does not solve the problem of the psychological imbalance. The Negro still remains, or is forced willy-nilly by this legalism to present himself as a petitioner. He remains in the humiliating position of asking whites to accept him, want him, like him. And to drop once and for all this *niaiserie* about intermarriage, what this imbalance really destroys is the basis of mutual respect and civil contact between equals.

So much for the doctrinaire individualism that has been one of the two extreme positions brought into being by the post-*Plessy* collapse. The other has been the doctrinaire nationalism that has ranged from Garvey to the Black Muslims. This has reasserted the idea of community but with an anti-white militancy that puts it out of range of the charge of "accommodation." The Black Muslims have been called many things but hardly "Uncle Toms." The common theme binding together this stream of protest is the view that the Negro will never get civic equality in a white man's country and that to gain respect he must either leave it, separate himself within it, or dominate it. Just as the first position, for all its tendencies toward self-depreciation, held sight of a crucial need and right of the American Negro, so does this second stream of protest, for all its bitterness, similarly have a grasp upon some important needs of the Negro. To the fact that the Negro does not have a moral community, they have asserted that this is so because the Negro is not committed to being a

Negro and that it is within the Negro's own powers to recover his pride. But they have responded not with a community but with a sect. To the fact that the Negro feels dependent upon white standards of approval, they have asserted the psychological and moral importance of inward self-sufficiency and independence. But they have responded with resentment and counterracism. Yet, is a Negro inwardly free if he feels less free to straighten his hair than a white person does to blacken himself in the sun? Finally, to the fact that the Negro does not have a culture of his own, they have sensed the disadvantage to which this puts the Negro. But then their response is to invent a culture proclaiming a fictitious identity.

The problem thus facing Negro leadership in the future is whether it can rejoin on a rational level the two goals of a moral community and civic equality that have been separated into these two extremes. Only in this way can it genuinely learn something from the experience of the nationalist stream of protest. Specifically, the question facing the Negro is whether he can develop a policy which recognizes these facts. First, it is only through the formation of a voluntary community that the Negro can be assimilated and that the kind of "interrace"-consciousness produced by the psychological imbalance discussed above would diminish. Second, if the community is to be a voluntary one, this implies that the Negro must be free to leave it; but freedom of this sort that is based on consent, if it is to be effective, must be exercised with self-restraint. Finally, if a community is to be a genuine community, it must possess some basis of inward cohesion, something approximating a "culture," which transcends mere race-consciousness. In short, the Negroes, if they are to acquire equality in more than merely a legal sense but in the sense of equal respect, must transform themselves into a people with sufficient pride so that they will be wooed. White society can and indeed must play a crucial role in sustaining the kind of fabric which in giving the Negro relief from public indignity and injustice would support a voluntary community. But the primary role in all this must be played by Negroes themselves. This flows from the fundamental fact that the self-sufficiency which is an element in genuine pride can never be acquired merely from opinions of another or of oneself, but depends, rather, upon objective achievements. Unless the standards of excellence or craftsmanship are present as controlling criteria in the kind of life one wants to lead, the quest for self-respect could crumble into "other-directed" vanity or resentment on the one hand or "inner-directed" delusions of grandeur on the other hand.

We conclude with a brief notation of some general details. On the level of social action the broad problem is the manifestation by Negroes to themselves that they have some responsibility for and some power to control the life in their own communities. This obviously lies within limits posed by the fact that a community of this sort does not and will not possess economic or political autonomy. Negroes, for example, no more than the municipalities as a whole in which they live, cannot control the problem of who and how many in-migrants are coming to the city from other parts of the country. Mr. Muhammad of the Black Muslims could instruct one of his sectarians, whose relatives had recently moved in from the South, to tell them that they would have to leave his apartment as they were overcrowding it and disturbing his own family life which was his primary responsibility. This simple and tough solution to demographic problems, whatever one may think of it, is hardly feasible for a community as a whole. But within the limits set by the fact that a community does not possess the autonomy which only a self-governing country has, the problem is to find those interstitial spheres where some latitude for autonomous civic action is possible. Urban redevelopment, with regard not merely to public but also to private housing developments, and the problem of securing upgraded levels of employment are two spheres where Negro leadership could evoke effort toward badly needed goals and in a manner which makes clear the legitimate interdependence between the Negro community and the rest of society. While a voluntary community is humiliated by imposed segregation which has the effect of keeping it at the status of a compulsory ghetto, the apprehensions of whites that Negroes moving into an area will "take it over" is connected not merely with irrational fear but with the knowledge that Negroes do not have an equivalent choice in a Negro district. The redevelopment of Negro physical communities and the disappearance of barriers to the Negro's residential mobility would thus mutually reinforce each other in a positive way. By the same token the existence of job ceilings which exclude Negroes who have made the effort to acquire qualifications for skilled jobs poisons the whole atmosphere of Negro society by making them look like fools in the eyes of those who are too demoralized to make efforts. The effect of exclusionist practices is thus to bring into prominence the voice within Negro society of the demoralized and the esteem of those who are admired by this stratum; that is, those with "flashy" money and with power based on "shady" activities within the Negro world, such as policy kings. The dissolution of this stratification is thus a most urgent prerequisite for the formation of a Negro community and, since Negroes cannot work in an independent Negro economy, one which calls for the exertion of every form of moral, legal, and political pressure and even economic power as Negroes discover what they collectively possess in these respects. But then this imposes duties upon Negro leadership to control the problem of drop-outs in high school and the whole problem of urban demoralization. These two things, once again, can only go hand in hand.

But what of the inwardness binding such a community? Can the Negro possibly have a culture? We have seen in the case of the sects.where the quest for a culture can lead, which is as much to confirm the view that the Negro has no culture or traditions of his own and that every effort to assert the contrary can lead him only to an absurd mystique of one sort or another. But implicit in the view that the Negro has no culture is the conception of culture as essentially focused upon a distinctive religion, taking shape within a distinct and autonomous political entity, in a society with its own distinctive language, all comprising an organic whole. This is, in short, a culture of a people or a folk, which may well be the original meaning of the term "culture"—which of all terms in the social scientist's vocabulary has certainly experi-

enced the greatest degree of evisceration. In this sense
of the term, the Negro has no culture of his own; but
then neither do many other people in the twentieth century whose "cultures" are penetrated by cosmopolitan
science and technology, ideologies, political ideas. The
question that then arises is whether the Negro, though
lacking a culture in this sense or something that is
derivative from such a culture, still possesses some cultural elements in common that are sufficiently distinctive to
be able to give him the basis for some kind of inner cohesion. The argument that the Negro lost his African
culture and, hence, has nothing which is not derivative
from or dependent upon white culture is ultimately mis-
leading. For what this point of view does is to elevate
the importance of the genesis of something to such a degree that it loses sight of the importance of the result.
Granted that the Negro began his experience in this
country in complete subordination to the white man's
language and ideas, this has not prevented him from
interacting with this out of his experience in his genuinely
unique situation to produce, if not a culture, a *style* that
is his own. It comes through in the very way in which the
nationalistic sects deny that they are Negroes. When the
Black Muslims say, "It is not the Negroes but the whites
who are a race because the whites are racing with time,"
this selected conjunction of irrelevancies to make up something which is not at all irrelevant is something that no
white could do or do well unless he learned how from a
Negro. There are such things as Negro ways. The psychological problem of the Negro in America, however,
is that the mere assertion of this fact raises the specter of

racism. One has only to utter the term "Negro mentality" to see where the matter really stands.

Mr. James Baldwin, in a provocative article, has stated that the Negro, out of his situation, is the only one in America who sees the truth behind the myths that white men believe and as such has a moral contribution to make to the perfection of his country.[10] Perhaps. But what he fails to say is that the Negro has lost the self-confidence to see the truth about himself. I say lost rather than never possessed because I believe Washington, who was at home with plantation Negroes and their humor as well as with educated Negroes and whites throughout the world, and who was altogether proud to be a Negro, possessed this. But the scar left by the letdown has been great, indeed. Out of this has come a loss of his capacity to turn inward, to reflect on his experience without resentment, and even to suspect that he may have something worthwhile of his own to hold onto. Yet, until this is clarified, how can a Negro decide with self-respect what he should assimilate to? White standards, but which ones? Perhaps he might become aware of the fact that there are certain standards he holds valuable which white men or all men might adopt. Precisely how this inward reorientation is to be brought about and what would be the result is something the Negro will have to find out for himself because it is a thing that only he can do. I would call it a creative reinterpretation of his experience that could lead to some kind of creative discovery.

As has been stated throughout this whole analysis, the role of white society in sustaining the kind of social and political fabric that would support the Negro's quest for self-respect is indispensable. The essence of this fabric is what I would call an open alliance between those whites and those Negroes who stand for excellence or the spirit of craftsmanship. I do not believe this would bring into existence in the practical future a society that would be as blind to the mere fact of color as would its Constitution and public law. But it would bring about a situation in which color was subordinated to qualifications. The active recognition of the obligation imposed upon whites to enable and to encourage Negroes to pursue these with dignity would be the repayment of the unpaid debt the United States owes the Negro, who was, indeed, as the Black Jews correctly say, robbed of his self-respect. But in a fundamental sense he can only recover this by himself. And this, I conclude, is the lesson to be learned from these very strange sects.

NOTES

CHAPTER I

1. E. Franklin Frazier, *The Negro in the United States* (New York: The Macmillan Company, 1949), p. 87.

2. For these details and a good description of the philo-Biblical and philo-Jewish atmosphere of seventeenth-century England, see Cecil Roth, *A History of the Jews in England,* 2d ed. (Oxford: Oxford University Press, 1949), pp. 149ff., and Albert M. Hyamson, *A History of the Jews in England* (London: Chatto and Windus, 1908), pp. 164-165.

3. See Cecil Roth, ed., *Magna Bibliotheca Anglo-Judaica:* a Bibliographical Guide to Anglo-Jewish History (London: The Jewish Historical Society of England, 1937), sec. B. 17.

4. See Roth, *A History of the Jews in England, op. cit.,* p. 150.

5. See Ronald Matthews, *English Messiahs* (London: Methuen, 1936), pp. 85-126.

6. See Denis Saurat, *Blake and Modern Thought* (Glasgow: The Dial Press, 1929), p. 53. Akin to this was the Celtomania of the eighteenth century which, going even farther, reversed the whole problem and asserted that the Patriarchs were Druids.

7. Joseph Jacobs, "Anglo-Israelism," *The Jewish Encyclopedia.*

8. See Winston S. Churchill, *A History of the English Speaking Peoples* (London: Cassel and Company, 1956), Vol.

II, p. 214; A. S. P. Woodhouse, ed., *Puritanism and Liberty* (London: Dent, 1938).

9. Frazier, *op. cit.*, p. 343.

10. C. Vann Woodward, *Origins of the New South 1877-1913* (Baton Rouge: Louisiana State University Press, 1951), p. 352.

11. *Ibid.*

12. See below, pp. 83, 100f.

13. Booker T. Washington, *The Future of the American Negro* (Boston: Small, Maynard and Company, 1902), pp. 182ff.

14. A statement of Bishop Plummer quoted in Raymond J. Jones, *A Comparative Study of Religious Cult Behavior Among Negroes* (Washington: Howard University, 1939), p. 103.

15. *Ibid.*, pp. 100-104.

16. Arthur H. Fauset, *Black Gods of the Metropolis* (Philadelphia: University of Pennsylvania Press, 1944), p. 37.

17. *Ibid.*, pp. 31-40.

18. See C. Eric Lincoln, *The Black Muslims in America* (Boston: Beacon Press, 1961), p. 11.

CHAPTER II

1. *New York Herald Tribune,* April 7, 1947, p. 5.

CHAPTER III

1. Edward Ullendorf, *The Ethiopians, an Introduction to Country and People* (London: Oxford University Press, 1960), p. 111.

2. "Ethiopia," and "Falashas," *Encyclopaedia Britannica,* 1947 ed.; Jacques Faitlovich, "The Falashas," *American Jewish Yearbook* (1920-21), Vol. XXII, pp. 80-100; "Falashas," *Jewish Encyclopedia.*

3. Ullendorf, *op. cit.*, pp. 111ff.

4. *Ibid.*, pp. 101, 103.

CHAPTER IV

1. Gunnar Myrdal, *An American Dilemma* (New York: Harper, 1944), p. 720.

2. See E. Franklin Frazier, *The Negro in the United States* (New York: The Macmillan Company, 1949), pp. 343-346.

3. Charles S. Johnson, *A Preface to Racial Understanding* (New York: Friendship Press, 1936), pp. 153ff.

4. See Albert P. Blaustein and C. C. Ferguson, *Desegregation and the Law* (New York: Vintage Books, 1962).

5. *Ibid.*, p. 98.

6. Cf. Myrdal, *op. cit.*, p. 208. "When slavery disappeared, caste remained."

7. William Graham Sumner, *Folkways* (Boston: Ginn and Company, 1906), p. 77. Italics not in the original.

8. See Henry V. Jaffa, *Crisis of the House Divided* (Garden City: Doubleday, 1959), p. 386.

9. C. Van Woodward, *The Strange Career of Jim Crow* (New York: Galaxy Books, 1957), p. 19.

10. *Ibid.*, p. 25.

11. W. E. B. DuBois, *The Souls of Black Folk* (Chicago: McClurg and Co., 1903), pp. 183-185.

12. C. Vann Woodward, *Origins of the New South* (Baton Rouge: Louisiana State University Press, 1951), p. 355.

13. Booker T. Washington, *Up From Slavery* (Garden City: Doubleday, Page, 1910), p. 202.

14. *Ibid.*, p. 109.

15. Booker T. Washington, *The Future of the American Negro* (Boston: Small, Maynard and Company, 1902), p. 158.

16. *Ibid.*, p. 148.

17. Washington, *Up From Slavery, op. cit.*, p. 221.

18. See Woodward, *The Strange Career of Jim Crow, op. cit.*, pp. 49-97. The impression, for example, given by Myrdal, *op. cit.*, pp. 739-742, among many other writers, is that Washington started his work after caste had become a settled fact. They simply failed to see the fluidity and the progress being made in the twenty years between the end of Reconstruction

and *Plessy* v. *Ferguson*. Here I believe Mr. Woodward's book contains wholly new insights which the earlier students did not possess.

19. Hampton M. Jarrell, *Wade Hampton and the Negro: The Road Not Taken* (Columbia, S. C.: University of South Carolina Press, 1950), pp. 121-124.

20. Woodward, *Origins of the New South, op. cit.,* p. 339.

21. Washington to Fortune, November 7, 1899, in Booker T. Washington Papers (Division of Manuscripts, Library of Congress), as quoted in Woodward, *Origins of the New South, op. cit.,* p. 338.

22. See DuBois, *op. cit.,* p. 43. In addition, the most vocal critics of Washington were opposed, if not to capitalism in a Marxist point of view, at least to capitalist culture and commercialism. To them Washington's emphasis on self-reliance was rank philistinism; and they had no hesitation in regarding his whole program at Tuskegee as suiting the self-interest of Northern businessmen. See DuBois, *loc. cit.* See also the forceful but historically wild indictment of Washington made by Kelly Miller in *Race Adjustment* (New York: 1910), pp. 19-20 (quoted in Frazier, *op. cit.,* pp. 545-546). Certainly Washington's policy was identical with that of Douglass, whom he regarded as a model and teacher. Contrary to Miller's explicit statement, they both spoke about rights in a democracy, as well as duties or qualifications. They both saw the issue of economic independence for the Negro in the same way. After the Civil War Douglass was busy encouraging Negroes to pursue scientific agriculture. But he had been exhorting them to elevate themselves by learning trades as early as 1848. To be sure, he was the leading Negro abolitionist. But then slavery existed; and, as Washington pointed out, once this evil was excised, the *emphasis* in policy had to be upon construction. See Howard Brotz, *Negro Social and Political Thought 1850–1920* (New York: Basic Books, 1966), pp. 203–208, 284–297, 382–396.

23. Claude McKay, *Harlem: Negro Metropolis* (New York: E. P. Dutton and Co., 1940), p. 176.

24. See above, p. 8.

25. W. E. B. DuBois, *Black Folk: Then and Now* (New York: Henry Holt, 1939), p. vii.

26. *Ibid.*, pp. 21-23. Italics not in the original.

27. *Ibid.*, p. 92.

28. *Ibid.*, p. 99.

29. Melville J. Herskovits, *The Myth of the Negro Past* (New York: Harper, 1942), pp. 1f.

30. Frazier, *op. cit.*, pp. 3-21.

31. *Ibid.*, p. 92.

32. Stanley Elkins, *Slavery* (Chicago: University of Chicago Press, 1959), p. 38.

33. *Ibid.*, pp. 37-80.

34. Kenneth M. Stampp, *The Peculiar Institution: Slavery in the Ante-Bellum South* (New York: Knopf, 1956), p. 76.

35. *Ibid.*, p. 43.

36. Frank Tannenbaum, *Slave and Citizen, the Negro in the Americas* (New York: Knopf, 1947), pp. 48, 54f.

37. Stampp, *op. cit.*, p. 141.

38. A good sketch of the evolution of the racial-slave status in law is to be found in Frazier, *op. cit.*, pp. 22-28. He cites a statement of John H. Russell that the year 1682 was "the upper limit of the period in which it was possible for Negroes to come to Virginia as servants and acquire freedom after a limited term." *Ibid.*, p. 26.

39. South Carolina in 1740 (as did also Georgia and Mississippi) ruled that "All negroes, Indians (those now free excepted) . . . mulattoes, or mestizos, who are or shall hereafter be in the province, and all their issue and offspring, born or to be born, shall be and they are hereby declared to be and remain forever hereafter absolute slaves and shall follow the condition of the mother." Cited in George M. Stroud, *A Sketch of the Laws Relating to Slavery in the Several States of the United States of America*, 2d ed. (Philadelphia: H. Longstreth, 1856), pp. 60-61.

40. Quoted in Blaustein and Ferguson, *op. cit.*, p. 84.

41. See Stampp, *op. cit.*, pp. 156, 158.

42. Cf. note 39 above.

43. See Stampp, *op. cit.*, p. 216.

44. See Stampp's discussion of infantilism among slaves. *Ibid.*, p. 327.

45. See Elkins, *op. cit.*, pp. 81-85. See also Stampp, *op. cit.*, p. 99.

46. Stampp notes that in slavery the slaves were rarely capitally punished by the state for murdering another slave. See *ibid.*, p. 227. See also John Dollard's discussion of this double standard of justice in his *Caste and Class in a Southern Town* (New Haven: Yale University Press, 1937), pp. 279-285.

47. The best study of Garvey is Edmund D. Cronon, *Black Moses: The Story of Marcus Garvey and the Universal Negro Improvement Association* (Madison: The University of Wisconsin Press, 1955).

48. *Ibid.*, p. 189.

49. Speech of Marcus Garvey delivered at Third International Convention of Peoples of African Blood and Descent, n.d.

50. There seems to be almost no continuity between the colonization programs of such pre-Civil War Negro leaders as John Russwurm and Edward Blyden and the twentieth-century developments. When Garvey arrived on the scene, Jewish Zionism, of course, was very much in the atmosphere.

51. See Cronon, *op. cit.*, p. 131.

52. See, for example, the interpretation in Myrdal, *op. cit.*, p. 749.

53. E. Franklin Frazier, *Black Bourgeoisie* (New York: The Free Press of Glencoe, 1957), p. 154.

54. See Cronon, *op. cit.*, p. 209.

55. Herbert Hill and Jack Greenberg, *Citizen's Guide to Desegregation: A Study of Social and Legal Change in American Life* (Boston: Beacon Press, 1955), pp. 31-36.

56. *Ibid.*, p. 33.

57. Myrdal, *op. cit.*, p. 814.

58. Two thorough studies of the Black Muslims are E. U. Essien-Udom, *Black Nationalism: A Search for an Identity in America* (Chicago: University of Chicago Press, 1962), and C. Eric Lincoln, *The Black Muslims in America* (Boston: Beacon Press, 1961).

59. See Erdmann D. Beynon, "The Voodoo Cult Among Negro Migrants in Detroit," *American Journal of Sociology*, XLIII (May, 1938), 894-907; Fauset, *op. cit.*, pp. 41-51.

60. Arthur H. Fauset, *Black Gods of the Metropolis* (Philadelphia: University of Pennsylvania Press, 1944), p. 47.

61. Beynon, *ibid.*

62. Lincoln, *op. cit.*, p. 75.

63. *Ibid.*, p. 68.

64. *Ibid.*, p. 20.

65. Essien-Udom, *op. cit.*, p. 112.

66. Mr. Essien-Udom believes that the extent of this aspect of the sect's work, because of its sensational character, is exaggerated out of all proportion and that the moral tone of the sect in fact makes for a self-selection among the new recruits, of people who are inclined toward self-restraint. See *ibid.*, p. 100.

67. *Ibid.*, p. 89.

CHAPTER V

1. This, for example, is the conclusion of C. Eric Lincoln, *The Black Muslims in America* (Boston: Beacon Press, 1961), pp. 254-255.

2. Booker T. Washington, *The Future of the American Negro* (Boston: Small, Maynard and Company, 1902), p. 148.

3. Cf. Gunnar Myrdal, *An American Dilemma* (New York: Harper, 1944), p. 927. By pathological, Myrdal meant not a condition of a Negro community at a particular time or place but, rather, its very existence. Akin to this is his understanding of race pride as resentment.

4. *Ibid.*, p. 469.

5. *Ibid.*, p. 76.

6. *Ibid.*

7. *Ibid.*, p. 11. Italics not in original.

8. James Q. Wilson, *Negro Politics* (New York: The Free Press of Glencoe, 1960), p. 5.

9. Donald Pierson, *Negroes in Brazil* (Chicago: The University of Chicago Press, 1942), p. 204.

10. James Baldwin, "Letter from a Region in My Mind," *The New Yorker*, November 17, 1962, pp. 142ff. Reprinted in *The Fire Next Time* (New York: The Dial Press, 1963), pp. 115ff.

INDEX OF NAMES